Data Structures

M. J. R. Shave, MA(Oxon), Ph. D. (Bristol)

Senior Lecturer in Computer Science,
University of Bristol

McGRAW-HILL Book Company (UK) Limited

London · New York · St Louis · San Francisco · Auckland · Beirut Bogotá
Düsseldorf · Johannesburg · Lisbon · Lucerne · Madrid · Mexico · Montreal
New Delhi · Panama · Paris · San Juan · São Paulo · Singapore · Sydney
Tokyo · Toronto

Published by
McGRAW-HILL Book Company (UK) Limited
MAIDENHEAD · BERKSHIRE · ENGLAND

Library of Congress Cataloging in Publication Data

Shave, M
   Data structures.

   (European computer science series)
   1. Data structures (Computer science) I. Title.
QA76.9.D35S47   001.6'4   75-22339
ISBN 0-07-084059-8

PRINTED AND BOUND IN GREAT BRITAIN

23456 JWA 8079

Typeset in Great Britain by
Preface Limited, Salisbury, Wilts
and printed in Great Britain by
J. W. Arrowsmith Limited, Bristol

To Ann, Susan and Peter

Contents

Preface

Computers were used at first only for solving numerical problems, but modern computer systems are applied to problems of a much more general character, such as the analysis of literary style, the construction of timetables, the retrieval of data from files and libraries, and the preparation of perspective drawings. The solution of these problems depends on the analysis and rearrangement of information associated with each problem. Clearly this information must be represented in a manner which a computer system can accept, but before deciding on a *method* of representation a more fundamental question is the *content* of the information — just *what* facts about the problem does the information convey? This may seem obvious, but consider the three symbols 'bow': these can be regarded as just three letters which determine a position in an alphabetical index, or as a word associated with a ship, or with music, or with formal ceremonial, or with archery.

In this case the context will soon clarify the meaning, but it is not always possible to determine which aspects of information are important. For example, suppose there is a list containing the names and addresses, occupations, and employers of a number of people: should this information be arranged in order of employee name (for tax collection), or occupation (for an employment agency), or employer's name (for a business register)? If the list is to serve more than one purpose, how can all these distinct relationships be represented? Are there any other orderings inherent in the information which may be the subject of an enquiry based on these data, and if so, should they also be represented? What steps can or should be taken to maintain each ordered relationship as names are added or deleted, or as companies merge or occupations are reclassified? These questions lead to consideration of ways in which the structure as well as the static content of information can be represented in a computer system — the relationships of data as well as their values. The relationships may themselves be static, such as the connection between the Centigrade and Fahrenheit measures of temperature, or they may change as the solution of a problem develops, as when constructing a timetable or analysing a sentence.

This book discusses the representation, description, use, and modification of structural aspects of information in terms which are largely independent of any specific area of application. It is suitable for any students who have taken a first course in Computer Science at college or university level and gained some experience of programming, preferably in a high-level language. Algol W, a language developed from Algol 60. is used for the description of algorithms associated with structures, and a brief account of the most relevant aspects of Algol W is included in the book, but previous knowledge of Algol is not essential, and readers with experience of other high-level languages should find the examples straightforward to follow.

The first two chapters make an important distinction between natural structures which are inherent, though rarely explicit, in almost every set of data, and any further relationships or restrictions which are created in order to represent the natural structure in a finite and inflexible computer store. Chapters 4—6 describe the basic operations applicable to stored structures, the allocation of storage for structures which can change dynamically, the representation and modification of tabular information — a particularly common form of structure — and the use of auxiliary storage for large files of data. Chapter 7 makes a comparative survey of the features relevant to structures in a number of programming languages which have varied characteristics and objectives, and in the final chapter there is a more general view of the representation of information, particularly in relation to the increasing use of large integrated data banks.

I should like to express my thanks to Professor M. H. Rogers, Mr F. G. Duncan and Mr J. A. Ogden who between them read all of the book in draft form and made many valuable suggestions for its improvement. Also to Brighton Polytechnic, City of Leicester Polytechnic, Queen Mary College of the University of London, and the Universities of Cambridge, Essex, Glasgow, and St Andrews, who kindly gave permission for some of their recent examination questions to be used as exercises in this book.

M. J. R. Shave

1. Natural structures in data

What is information?

It is easy to give examples of information, but much less so to frame a formal definition, because the word describes a concept and not an object. Information is associated with an attribute or a set of attributes of a situation or an object: the number of people in a room, the size of a book, the colour and make of a car. But to transmit and use these abstract properties they are *represented* in some way (by a word such as 'green' or by a measure on an agreed scale) and these representations *convey* the information or knowledge. As a result of frequent and well-understood use, these representations come to be accepted as *being* the information they convey; the distinction between the abstract attributes and their representation is unimportant, except when it is necessary to consider alternative methods of representation. In this way the symbols 20, 10100 (binary scale), and XX all convey the same information about the century in which this book has been written.

When talking about information we often say that we wish 'to obtain (or give) information about . . .', and this phrase emphasizes both the association of information with a specific thing and also the communication involved. We might ask whether information exists when it is *not* transmitted. For instance we can describe a painting and thereby convey information about it, but is the painting itself 'information'? This is perhaps a philosophical question, and for our present purposes we can say that information is 'stored' in the painting in the sense that its attributes do not change (except perhaps its value!), and therefore the same information about it could be given on two different occasions. We will restrict the discussion of information to cases in which it is transmitted, or stored for later transmission; and since this book is not about language or communication theory but about the use of computer systems, we shall be particularly concerned with methods of storing information.

Structure as a property of data

Everyone uses information every day. Much of the information is so familiar that we hardly realize we are using it, such as the address where we live, or a familiar cookery recipe, or how to use a telephone; this is information which we have learnt and retained. On other occasions it is necessary to find out the information we need — for example, when we use a telephone directory or a timetable — but notice that we still have to know where to *start* looking for the answers we want. When faced with any problem we cannot find a solution unless we can decide

what we wish to know,
where the information can be found, and
how it is to be obtained.

In the case of a telephone number, once we have the correct directory we can find a particular number by knowing that the names of all subscribers are listed in alphabetical order. This illustrates a very important feature of information namely, that it usually involves not only a set of *values* but also a *structure* which connects the values in some way.

The alphabetical structure of the telephone directory has been chosen in order to make reference easy, but it is by no means the only structure associated with this set of information. The entries could have been listed in the order of the telephone numbers, an arrangement which might be more convenient for the Post Office when allocating numbers or billing subscribers. Or again, entries could be listed by streets, with the streets listed alphabetically, or by districts; this would create a 'multi-level directory', and to find the telephone number of 'A. Smith, 15 Station Road, Hightown', we should search first for 'Hightown', then within this section for 'Station Road', and finally for No. 15 in this street.

The structure of the telephone directory has been imposed on it for ease of use. In other cases, the structure of data may occur as a natural part of the meaning which the data convey: the members of a football team, for example, are stated in four groups according to their role on the field. To obtain the name of the goalkeeper, we would look at the first name on the list; for the left wing we would look at the last name in the fourth group of players. The names of all the members of a family form another example of structured data: if we think of all the descendants of a particular individual, the structure is basically a 'tree' with a number of disjoint 'branches', each of which itself has a tree structure. In a very closed society or over several generations, intermarriages may occur which make the form of the data more complex.

Weight not over	1st class post	2nd class post
2 oz	7p	5½p
4 oz	10p	8p
6 oz	12½p	9½p
8 oz	15p	11p
10 oz	17½p	13p

Fig. 1.1   Postal rates

	Birmingham	Bristol	Edinburgh	Glasgow	Leeds	London	Manchester	Newcastle
Birmingham								
Bristol	87							
Edinburgh	286	365						
Glasgow	287	365	44					
Leeds	109	194	191	210				
London	110	116	373	392	190			
Manchester	79	159	210	211	40	184		
Newcastle	200	284	106	143	91	273	128	

Fig. 1.2   Mileage chart

   The alphabetic ordering of a telephone directory is easily recognized, but in cases where the ordering is less obvious, the data may be shown diagrammatically. A common situation is one in which the data can be shown as a table or 'rectangular array': in Fig. 1.1 each unit of information consists of three values, with cost dependent on weight and class of post, and consequently a two-dimensional representation is particularly convenient. The data in Fig. 1.2 could similarly have been presented in a square format, but mileages are inherently symmetrical and therefore in this case it is sufficient, and more economical, to use only the lower-triangular subset of the complete structure.

   These examples all illustrate the essential fact that information has order as well as value. Often the structure remains constant, and it is only the values within it that change: for instance, the categories of delivery and weights in Fig. 1.1 will alter rarely, but the corresponding charges change frequently. In other cases a change in data values may cause a change in the data structure. Consider a table which shows the points won by teams in a football league (2 points for a win, 1 for a draw): if the table is arranged alphabetically, then the result of a match cannot alter the order, but if — as is more usual — the teams are arranged by the number of points they have gained, then their order is liable to change whenever their points totals are updated. It is also possible to alter a data structure without changing any values, as when a car-hire firm keeps records of all its cars arranged by the area to which they are assigned; a reallocation of

Structure	Access algorithm
Set of instructions numbered sequentially	Read instruction 3.
Rectangular table of values	Read the value in row x and column y, where x and y are known integer values.
Alphabetical list of names and addresses	Compare required name with the name in the middle of the list; if required name is 'earlier' in the alphabet, repeat this rule with upper half list; if 'later' in the alphabet, repeat with lower half list; continue until comparison yields an exact match, or there is total failure.

Fig. 1.3

cars means a reorganization of records, but does not affect the technical details of their fleet in any way. (Note: we could regard 'home base' as a value within a record rather than a direction for entering the structure. In this sense a change of base would entail a change of value as well as order.)

Whatever the purpose of a set of data, the first necessity is to be able to reach at will any item of the set, that is, we require an access rule or 'algorithm'. Clearly it is desirable for this rule to be as simple as possible, for this is likely to lead to the greatest efficiency in its operation; it must, however, be able to cope with any changes in the structure of the data, and in all cases it must be precise. 'Find the smallest item in the given set of data' would not be acceptable, because this begs the question of *how* to find the smallest item. Some possible algorithms applicable to fixed data structures are shown in Fig. 1.3.

When the data structure is not fixed, the access rule must correspondingly be more flexible, and it is usually necessary to describe in more detail how to move from one element in the structure to another since, by hypothesis, the ordering of the elements is not predictable in advance. A typical problem is to find the playing record of a particular football club in a league: the leading club is indicated by an initial pointer, and thereafter a succession of pointers corresponding to the playing order leads to each club in turn until the search is successful. This may seem a laborious method, but it is important to recognize that the objective is to develop algorithms which are applicable to very large data structures. In very limited cases it may be possible to take an overall glance at a set of elements and pick out one which has a distinctive characteristic, but when the set is of any significant size, the data must be examined systematically, element by element. This is a further reason why access algorithms must be precise.

Operations on structures
We introduced an example in which it is necessary to rearrange a structure when we discussed the ordering of a set (or *list*) of football teams. This task also

4

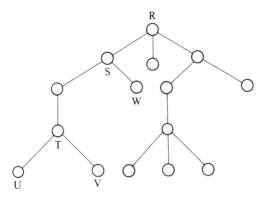

Fig. 1.4   A tree structure

involves *tracing* all the elements on a list, and other common operations on such a structure are the addition or deletion of an element, and the joining or *concatenation* of two lists. To carry out these operations, it is necessary to have a clear definition of the format of each element in a structure: for example, each entry in a telephone directory involves three items or *fields* — a name, an address, and a number — and the size and convention for writing each of these must be carefully stated.

These basic operations of definition, tracing, ordering, and updating are also applicable to more complex structures, but their execution is correspondingly more complicated. To take just one example at this stage, consider how to trace all the elements in a tree structure such as Fig. 1.4. Starting from the root R we must consider the branches in some logical order (such as left to right in the diagram) and scan systematically down the chosen branch until a terminal element, e.g. U, is reached. This will define a unique and non-repetitive trace since, by definition, each branch itself has the structure of a tree and hence the tracing algorithm can be applied recursively from the subroot S and similar points. However, in carrying out the trace it is necessary to remember any root or subroot where there is still a branch to be traced — for example, S and T must be remembered while tracing U, so that V and W can later be found. This problem will be discussed in more detail in chapter 4, and this brief summary merely indicates some of the additional problems which arise when considering structures more complex than a simple list.

Classification of structures

Technical jargon is frequently criticized, and rightly so, when it is used without adequate explanation and leads to the unnecessary confusion of the layman. By contrast, the clear definition of some technical terms can avoid lengthy phraseology, and thereby clarify the description of a subject, and this is the objective of the following classification of a number of important and common information structures. We take the idea of a *set* of items to be intuitive, and will use the term *alphabet* to refer to a finite set of symbols, e.g. all symbols on a standard typewriter, or all digits, or all symbols available on an IBM 029 card punch. Note that space can be a symbol of an alphabet. In describing structures it will not usually be necessary to specify a particular alphabet.

A *string* is an ordered set of symbols from some alphabet. Some examples are:

aeiou
125478
+–*/=
THIS TOO IS A STRING
& 5 > enough!

The constituent symbols of a string can be quite unrelated; the *length* of a string is the number of symbols which it contains. Any rearrangement of a given string is regarded as a distinct string, thus

aeiou   is distinct from   eoiau

A string which contains no symbols is called an *empty string*, has length zero, and is denoted by ∧. This concept can be useful in avoiding the need to state special cases, and plays a similar role to the zero in arithmetic, or the null set in set theory.

A *vector* is an ordered set of values. The values are generally, but not necessarily, numbers and the most familiar example is a vector which defines the position of a point in a plane, or a point in space. The term may also be used to refer to the contents of a set of locations or addresses which define the representation of a structure in a computer store.

It is an essential feature of a vector that all its constituent elements must be

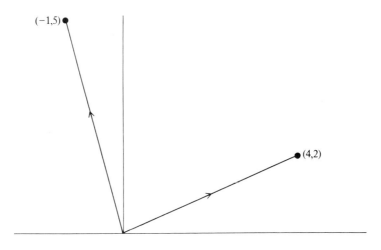

Fig. 1.5   The points represented by vectors (4,2) and (−1,5)

6

of the same type, e.g., all real numbers, or all logical values. The *size* of a vector is the number of elements it contains.

An alternative name for a vector is an *array of one dimension*, because a single subscript value is sufficient to identify any one of the elements forming the vector. An *array of n dimensions* is a natural extension of the concept of a vector. For example, if the coordinate axes in a plane are rotated anticlockwise through an angle θ, the transformation to be applied to the coordinates of any point in the plane is described by the real-valued, two-dimensional array

$$\begin{pmatrix} \cos\theta & \sin\theta \\ -\sin\theta & \cos\theta \end{pmatrix}.$$

If, after rotation, the origin is moved distances α and β in the new x and y directions respectively, then the transformation as a whole can be described by the two-dimensional array

$$\begin{pmatrix} \cos\theta & \sin\theta & -\alpha \\ -\sin\theta & \cos\theta & -\beta \end{pmatrix}.$$

In a similar way, a two-dimensional array containing logical values can indicate whether it is possible to pass directly between a number of given points: a 'true' value in position (i, j) shows that a direct path exists from i to j and Fig. 1.6(b) is the array which corresponds to the set of paths shown in Fig. 1.6(a). Notice that two subscript values are necessary to identify an element belonging to a two-dimensional array.

Remember that all the elements of an array must be of the same type (real numbers, logical values, etc.) and that the number of elements in any chosen direction is normally constant, but the size in one direction need not be the same as the size in another. (For example, an array of three dimensions has the shape of a rectangular brick.) Formally, we can define an *array of n dimensions* as an ordered set of arrays each of $n - 1$ dimensions, each having elements of the

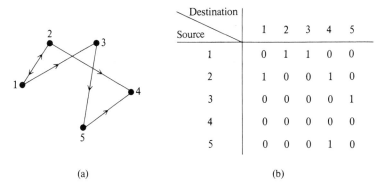

Source \ Destination	1	2	3	4	5
1	0	1	1	0	0
2	1	0	0	1	0
3	0	0	0	0	1
4	0	0	0	0	0
5	0	0	0	1	0

(a)   (b)

Fig. 1.6   A two-dimensional logical array used to indicate feasible paths

same type, and each having the same sizes in corresponding dimensions; this recursive definition is meaningful because we obtain a vector when n = 1.

However, besides the fact that its elements must all be of a common type, the most important feature of any given array in the context of this chapter is that its structure remains constant and only its values are liable to change: e.g. the transformation of coordinates resulting from *any* rotation and/or translation of the plane is described by some 2 x 3 array having the form shown on p. 7.

A *record* is an ordered set of items which need not be all of the same type. For example, an entry in a telephone directory, or the information to be printed on an employee's payslip, or an item in a retail sales list. The non-homogeneity of a record distinguishes it from a vector.

A *table* associates a set of records which have a common format. Examples are:

1 a table of currency exchange rates
2 a table of high and low tide, and the height of the tide
3 a table of duties and the staff responsible for them.

A table is very similar in structure to a two-dimensional array, but there are a number of major differences:

(a) the elements of a table need not be of homogeneous type (e.g. (2) above) though any one entry (record) is consistent with another;
(b) the concept of ordering is not necessarily associated with a table (e.g. (3) above);
(c) the number of entries in a table may be subject to change.

When we consider the purpose of a table and of an array, there is the further distinction that a table contains information *about* objects, i.e. their properties, whereas an array more commonly contains values *applicable* to objects, i.e. it can operate on objects and transform them in some way.

Variable structures

In all the structures defined so far — string, vector, array, record and table — the elements have been associated with each other in a relatively inflexible way: if an element P lies between elements A and B, then this relationship remains true even though some value associated with P may change. In the structures now to be defined, the interrelationships of elements are as liable to change as are their values.

A *linear list* is a set of ordered pairs such that

1 every element of the list except one has a unique successor determined by the second item of the pair;
2 the first item of the pair is a value — numeric, logical, string, etc. — or a set ɔ̣. such values;

3 the exceptional (last) element of the list conventionally takes the value 'NULL' for its successor field;
4 a linear list can be empty, i.e. it can contain no elements.

Examples: a list of stops on a railway or airline route
        a list of clues found in a treasure hunt
        a route map.

A diagrammatic representation of the last example, showing each town and the route number necessary to reach the following town, is shown in Fig. 1.7.

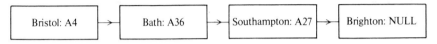

Fig. 1.7   Route map from Bristol to Brighton; a linear list

In some cases the second item of the ordered pair is implied rather than explicit. For example, we might construct a list of the definitions in a book, and state them in alphabetical order, or alternatively in the order of their introduction. In either case, the ordering of the elements on the list of definitions would be implied. However, a list constructed on a sequential basis such as this vitiates one of the most important features of a linear list, namely its adaptability to additions and deletions which occur randomly within it. It is an unfortunate fact that much of the information we use is printed and flexibility can be achieved only at the cost of reprinting. For this reason many data which should ideally be shown in the flexible format of a linear list with explicit successors are instead printed sequentially (e.g. a telephone directory), with any alterations made infrequently or contained in a supplementary list.

The flexibility of a list is the chief feature which distinguishes it from a vector. But note also that the elements of a list, unlike those of a vector, need not be of uniform type (though they frequently are), and that a list is still called linear even if the first item of each element is a set of values. Contrast this with the definition of an array of two dimensions.

A simple linear list can be described concisely by using parentheses: if such a list has five elements associated with the values A, B, C, D, E respectively, we can describe it by the expression

(A, B, C, D, E).

By using nested parentheses we can extend this notation to describe a *non-linear list*: suppose the element with value A is also associated with a linear list of three elements whose values are X, Y, Z and that D is associated with a linear list containing the values P, Q. We could describe this structure as

(A(X, Y, Z), B, C, D(P, Q), E).

A corresponding diagrammatic description is shown in Fig. 1.8.

The parentheses notation has some merits, particularly ease of printing, but it

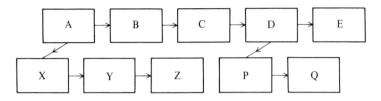

Fig. 1.8

cannot cope easily with more general structures such as those illustrated in Fig. 1.9.

Special linear lists

Despite the limitations of linear structures, a number of special linear lists are of particular importance in the study of data structures.

A *stack* is a linear list in which additions and deletions take place only at the beginning of the list. A moment's reflection will show that this means that only the most recently added element can be accessed and removed; for this reason a stack is also known as a *last-in, first-out list* or *LIFO list*. A set of items placed on a hook or spike demonstrates the principles of stack operations.

A common occurrence of this structure is in problems which involve 'looking ahead' for some condition or symbol, such as the evaluation of an arithmetic expression in which the priority of the operators must be considered. Another name for a stack is a 'pushdown list', from the manner in which a new element pushes existing elements of the list 'out of sight'. However, this is a misleading name, for a new element is placed in front of, or above, existing elements and does not cause any movement in the stack as a whole (see Fig. 1.10). Notice also that the deletion of an element from a stack (or any list) means that it is no longer relevant to the structure; this meaning must be clearly distinguished from an operation which replaces the existing *value* of an element by a zero or blank value. Both types of operation are applicable to list structures, but only the latter type applies to structures such as arrays.

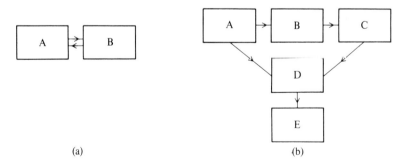

(a)   (b)

Fig. 1.9

10

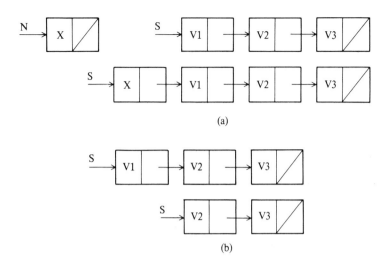

Fig. 1.10 Diagrammatic representation of operations on a stack S: (a) before and after addition of an element N, (b) before and after deletion of an element.

A *queue* is a linear list in which additions are made only at one end of the list (the 'rear') and deletions only at the other end (the 'front'). This is a *first-in, first-out (FIFO) list* since it is clear that an element, once added to the rear of the list, can be removed when and only when all earlier additions have been removed (consider the element with value V3 in Fig. 1.11).

When a receptionist makes a list of the names of patients who arrive to see a doctor, adding each new name at the foot of the list and crossing the top name

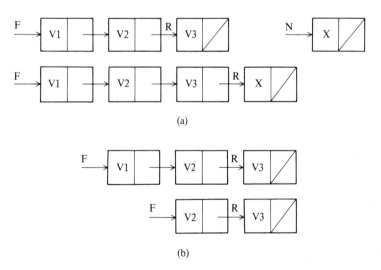

Fig. 1.11 Diagrammatic representation of operations on a queue, F: (a) addition of an element, N, (b) deletion of an element.

11

off the list as a patient is called in, her list of names has the structure of a queue. The word 'queue' is also used in many other everyday examples, such as the queue of traffic at a road junction, but it should be noted that in many cases (the traffic queue is one) the example is not a true queue, as the set of members moves up when one member is deleted. For a queue, as for a stack, the addition or deletion of an element need not affect any other elements of the list.

A *deque* is a linear list where additions and deletions may take place at either end of the list, but never in the middle. If input is restricted to one end, but output can take place at either end, we speak of an 'input-restricted' deque; an 'output-restricted' deque is similarly defined. A deque which is both input-restricted and output-restricted must be either a stack or a queue.

Variable non-linear structures

A surprising number of problems involve only linear structures, but in general more complex relationships will exist.

A *tree* is a set of elements such that one element (called the *root*) is the unique predecessor of all others, and the remaining elements, if any, form disjoint subsets, each of which is itself a tree. Unless otherwise stated, it will be assumed that the subsets can be ordered. Figure 1.4 illustrates this structure and examples occur in the traditional managerial structure of a company, in a family tree (provided there are no intermarriages), or in the classification of a subject for a catalogue. In Fig. 1.4, the element R is the root of the tree and there are three subtrees: the first (of which S is the root) contains six elements, the second has only one element, and the third has seven. U and V are roots of subtrees (or 'subroots') which have no further elements; U and V are known as 'terminal' or 'leaf' elements.

A *directed graph* or *digraph* is a set of elements some or all of which are joined by directed links or *arcs*. If P and Q are any two elements of the digraph, an arc may exist from P to Q, from Q to P, from P to itself, from Q to itself, or there may be any combination of these. Thus a digraph, unlike a tree, has no unique root, may contain loops and alternative paths, and possesses the more general concept of a path from one element to another in place of the concept of precedence. Figure 1.12 illustrates two digraphs, and good examples are formed by an airline route map, by a flowchart or project plan (where the elements are intermediate activities in the overall development), and by a 'state graph' which describes the transformations of a device which possesses a finite number of possible states or positions.

It may seem surprising to define only two types of non-linear structure, but it must be recognized that the digraph in particular is a very flexible and general concept. Not only may any element have any number of arcs leading to and from it, but in addition each element is a record and can contain any number of distinct values all of different types. Thus an element in Fig. 1.12(a) may contain a name (of the associated operation), two dates (earliest start and latest possible completion), a cost, a vector of manpower requirements, etc; in some

12

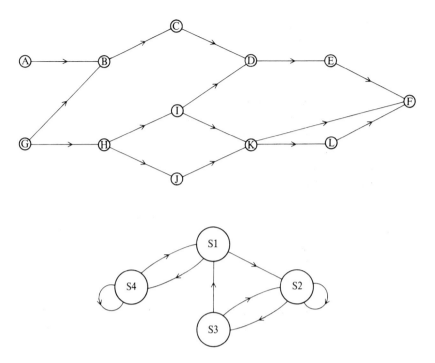

Fig. 1.12 Two digraphs: (a) a project plan; (b) a state graph.

cases these values may change without affecting the structural relationship (e.g., cost), in other cases a change of value may also cause a change of structure (e.g., dates).

Summary
Some items of information are totally unrelated — such as the boiling point of water, the colour of grass, and the price of flour! But any set of *related* information exhibits some form and degree of natural structure besides containing the values which are related.

In some situations, the structure is of constant shape and only the values within that structure change; a string, an array, and a table are normally of this type. In many other cases, the structure of the data is as variable as their values, and both are of equal importance: linear lists, trees, and digraphs are of this type, and the relationships between their elements must usually be stated explicitly, because the structures are too volatile to allow sequential orderings to describe them adequately.

Throughout this chapter we have discussed relationships which are *inherent* in sets of data. A closely related, equally important, but quite separate question is how to *represent* these inherent relationships when the data are stored (whether on paper, in a computer store, or any other medium). This problem of mapping

13

or transforming natural data structures into suitable *storage structures* is the subject of the next chapter.

Problems

1.1 This chapter has suggested that information

  must be associated with a situation or object

  has structure as well as value

  is communicable.

  Are all these properties necessarily present? Are there any other general properties of information?

1.2 Is information always represented or coded in some way when it is used? Does such coding impose restrictions on the information which is conveyed and, if so, does this matter? Should a man's name be regarded as a 'code' or as an attribute of the man? Similarly, how should today's date or the colour of grass be regarded?

1.3 Which of the structures defined in this chapter would be most appropriate to describe the following relationships? In each case explain your choice briefly.

   (a) the set of characters on a typewriter keyboard;
   (b) the catalogue of cars which are for sale at a garage;
   (c) the coefficients of a polynomial;
   (d) a set of monthly productivity statistics covering a period of one year;
   (e) a set of operating instructions for a piece of electrical or mechanical equipment;
   (f) a file of correspondence relating to a contract between a company and its customer.

1.4 A firm keeps records of its employees which include the employee's name, age, marital status, job or department title, date of appointment, salary grade, and tax code.

  Write down at least six ways in which these data are interrelated.

1.5 Suppose that a tree is traversed branch-by-branch as in Fig. 1.4, and that the maximum number of levels in any branch is L (L = 5 in Fig. 1.4). What is the maximum number of branch points which it may be necessary to remember at any one time? What is the corresponding maximum number if the value of L is unknown, but the tree is known to contain E elements in all?

1.6 Another systematic method of examining all the elements in a tree would be to look at them level by level instead of branch by branch. Does either method have significant advantages (a) in general, (b) for a specific practical application?

1.7 An array can have any number of dimensions, but there is no corresponding generalization of a table. Why is this? (Consider the relationship between elements in an array, and between field values in a table.)

1.8 An input device reads characters one at a time and each one is either placed on a stack or transmitted directly to an output stream. Verify that an input stream of two characters can be output in either order, but that it is possible to output only five of the six permutations of an input stream of three characters.
    If the stack is replaced by a queue, what difference would this make to the output?

1.9 Describe the primitive operations which may be performed on a linear list. In what way are these operations limited for (a) a stack, (b) a queue?
    Two stacks, p and q, contain nodes of identical structure ordered on a certain attribute, with the earliest values in the ordering being at the tops of the stacks. A third stack, r, is available and is initially empty. Show how it is possible to produce the complete ordered set of nodes in stack p, with the earliest value at the top.

(Glasgow, 1974)

1.10 A *postfix expression* is one in which an operator is placed *after* the operands to which it refers instead of the more familiar 'infix' notation. For example, B + C becomes BC+ in postfix form. If a sub-expression must be evaluated first, then this sub-expression (in postfix form) occurs in place of an operand, thus avoiding the need for brackets. For example,

(a) A + B * C becomes ABC*+ in postfix form
(b) (A + B) * (C + D) becomes AB+CD+* in postfix form.

    Given an algebraic expression such as (a) which involves only the four basic arithmetic operators, show how a stack can be used to convert this to postfix notation, assuming that a table is available giving the level of priority for each operator.
    What additional rules are necessary when the infix expression may contain brackets, as in (b)?
    Illustrate your answers by considering the expressions

(c) A + B * C – D / E
(b) A + B * (C + D * (E + F))

1.11 Show that an algebraic expression can be represented as a tree structure. Describe a systematic method of traversal of the tree which would lead to the output of the expression in postfix order. Illustrate your answer by considering the expressions (a) and (b) in the previous question and also the expression

$$(A + \sqrt{B})/(C + D * \sqrt{E})$$

1.12 Devise a non-pictorial method of describing a digraph (which could be used, for example, for computer input or output of digraph structures, using punched cards and lineprinter).

1.13 A building contains offices for staff and offices for secretaries; offices are equipped with telephones and furniture. Each staff member except one has another staff member as his superior, and each secretary is assigned to one or more staff members.

Design a data structure suitable to describe this information, and which can be used to answer the following types of question:

(a) How many people are more than three to an office and not on the same floor as their secretaries?
(b) What is the average number of desks per person in offices of people junior to Mr X?
(c) How many people does Mr Y's secretary look after? Is the secretary more than six floors away from any of them?

(Cambridge, 1973)

2. Storage structures

The previous chapter concentrated on the natural structures of data, but it was impossible to avoid introducing some representations of those structures: recall the diagrams which illustrated the chapter. This shows how one inevitably forms some model of a real-life system, in order to describe its characteristics concisely and to discuss operations which can be performed on it. One of the chief advantages in constructing such a model is that it enables us to concentrate on the representation of those features of the real-life situation which are pertinent to the problem in hand and ignore those which are irrelevant: for example, when considering a family tree, we are interested in names and relationships, but in general such items as the height, weight, or occupation of each member are not relevant.

Some data structures can be well represented by models similar to those built from children's constructional toys. Many readers may have seen models of chemical molecules like that shown in Fig. 2.1, and F. G. Duncan has shown that similar models can be built to correspond to the structure of a well-defined computer programming language. In this latter case the nodes represent the various statement forms and declarations of the language, and rods link an element of the language with sub-elements which are used in its definition.

Many types of models can be constructed; very often a mathematical model is used, more particularly when we are concerned with the values of a set of data but the structure is of little interest. Correspondingly, the examples of the previous chapter show the merits of diagrammatic models when the structure of data is of importance (and the total quantity of information to be represented is not too great). We could regard a diagram as a storage structure in the sense that both the values and the structure of a set of data can be incorporated within it. However, the capacity of a diagram is obviously severely limited and its chief value, apart from purposes of illustration, is to serve as a guide to the representation and storage of much larger volumes of data in machine-readable form, i.e., using punched cards, a fast core store in a computer, magnetic tapes, etc.

Similarly, the choice of a suitable computer model to represent a given set of data is influenced by the volume of data, and by such characteristics as the number of interrelationships and whether individual items are fixed or variable in length. But the most important factor is the use to be made of the data: how frequently, and in what context, will the items be required? For example, a

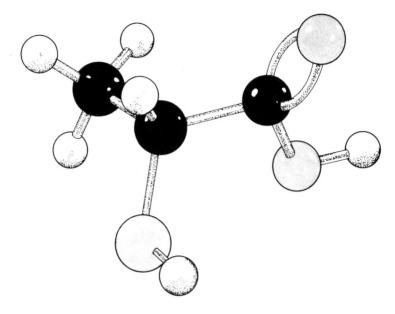

Fig. 2.1

telephone subscriber may wish to find the number of another subscriber whose name he knows, or the address of a friend with a commonly occurring surname whose telephone number he can remember, or the numbers of all the chemists' shops in his area. If enquiries of all these types may occur, how efficiently must answers be provided and which is the most critical? Furthermore, what changes may be made in the data while they are stored, and will these be changes of value or of structure or both? These are typical of the problems which must be considered when any storage structure is designed, and this and the following chapters will discuss how they are related to the choice of a method of implementation.

Machine-readable stores
Early forms of automatic information processing depended on mechanical techniques, and information was represented by holes punched in cards or in a reel of paper tape. The control cards of the Jacquard loom are the classic example of this form of machine-readable storage medium, and in a very different context the pianola illustrates the use of a paper-tape store. Both cards and paper tape are still used in conjunction with modern computers, but essentially only for communicating with the computer system at the input and output stages; their former role as 'on-line' storage, i.e. storage used at the time of processing, is no longer practicable, as a result of the vast increase in processing speeds which resulted from the introduction of electronic devices. To

link a computer directly to such slow mechanical media would be like using a very fast car when delivering letters to all the houses in a street.

As a result of the electronic operation of the modern computer, all information is stored in a binary form: that is to say, a suitable code, which uses only the binary alphabet, must be devised to represent every item of information which is relevant to a particular problem. Of course there are many possible codes: if we wish to use a simple number (e.g., to refer to a location in the store), all we need to do is to write that number in the binary scale — so that the eleventh location will be referred to as location 1011, the eighty-ninth location as location 1011001, and so on. To refer to symbols, a more arbitrary code must be used, and one of the most common is the EBCDIC code, of which a subset is shown in Fig. 2.2.

It must be recognized, however, that numbers and alphanumeric symbols are not the only entities which can be represented and stored. By choice of suitable binary codes, we can also store colours, musical notation, phonetic symbols, and many others — most of which also introduce the problem of representing interrelationships.

Whatever its physical construction, the traditional main store of a computer is logically a large one-dimensional vector, and any data possessing some other structure must be mapped or transformed into this linear format by a suitable function whose domain is the set of data (including both value and structure),

Binary code	Decimal value	Character	Binary code	Decimal value	Character
0100 0000	64	(space)	1100 0001	193	A
			1100 0010	194	B
			:		:
0100 1011	75	.	1100 1001	201	I
0100 1100	76	<			
0100 1101	77	(	1101 0001	209	J
0100 1110	78	+	1101 0010	210	K
			:		:
0101 1100	92	*	1101 1001	217	R
0101 1101	93	)			
0101 1110	94	;	1110 0010	226	S
1000 0001	129	a	1110 0011	227	T
:		:	:		:
1000 1001	137	i	1110 1001	233	Z
1001 0001	145	j	1111 0000	240	0
:		:	1111 0001	241	1
1001 1001	153	r	1111 0010	242	2
			:		:
1010 0010	162	s	1111 1001	249	9
:		:			
1010 1001	169	z			

Fig. 2.2   A subset of the EBCDIC character codes (Extended Binary-Coded Decimal Interchange Code)

and whose range is a subset of the storage vector. The concept of the store as a linear vector is initially due to Von Neumann; alternative hardware can permit a different interpretation of the store in which, for example, different types of variable occupy distinct areas of store, or the user can define 'segments' to simplify the representation of the structure of his data. Practical progress in this direction has been slow (Iliffe, 1972).

In most computer systems, economic considerations enforce the use of a hierarchy of stores in which the major capacity is not available for random access. It is then necessary to consider the physical location of related blocks of information, as much time can be wasted in transferring data to and from main and auxiliary store, and also in excessive disc-head movement or tape winding. The structure of files of data held in auxiliary storage will be discussed in chapter 6, but any reorganization of data must normally be carried out in the main store. Hence the main emphasis is placed in this book on the representation and manipulation of structures in a fast random-access store.

Sequential storage structures

All computer hardware has provision for 'instruction modification' — that is, facilities which enable the location on which an instruction operates to be altered by a program during its execution. These instructions are very efficient in operation and by systematic modification it is possible to obtain easy access to a regular pattern of locations; in particular, to a sequential set of locations. As a consequence, it is very convenient to use a sequential area for a storage structure if a mapping can be devised which enables the corresponding data structure to be represented in this way.

A vector is particularly amenable to this form of representation, for three reasons:

1   it is naturally one-dimensional;
2   its elements are homogeneous in type;
3   its structure is fixed, though the values within that structure may change.

To store a vector, a block of nk bytes is set aside, where k is the uniform size needed to store one element and n is the number of elements; then access to the qth element $(q = 0, 1, \ldots, n - 1)$ can be made immediately by placing q in the index register in conjunction with the appropriate instruction.

If any of the three characteristics above is not present, a sequential storage structure is to some extent inconvenient, but the advantages in economy of space and in convenience of access may still outweigh the disadvantages of an inflexible format. (3) is the crucial factor, because when a structure changes (e.g., one new element is added), the inherent ordering of the sequential storage structure no longer corresponds to the natural order of the data structure unless or until a *set* of elements has been relocated (Fig. 2.3).

Even when data elements are homogeneous (criterion (2)), problems occur if they vary in length, that is, in the amount of space required to store each

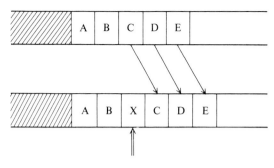

Fig. 2.3 The addition of the element X to the sequential structure causes changes in other positions

element when its value is represented in a suitable code. Note first that 'length' is not synonymous with 'value': the strings 'ABC' and 'DEF' have the same length but different values; by contrast the numbers 15.0 and 15.0000 have different lengths but (for many purposes) the same value. 'Floating point' or 'scientific' notation (in which numbers are written in the form a x power of 2 or 10, where a lies in a standard range such as $0.1 \leqslant a < 1$) enables a fixed length to be used for the storage of numerical data, whilst ensuring that the vital digits of each number are kept.

If all elements of a sequentially stored set have the same length, then any one element can be accessed by an increment proportional to its position in the set, but this is not possible with data of variable length (for example, a set of postal

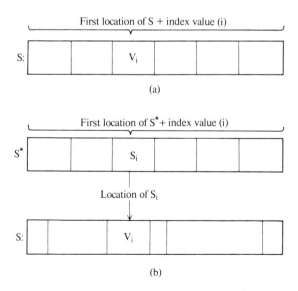

Fig. 2.4 Access to sequential storage: (a) fixed length data (b) variable length data

21

addresses). One solution, which preserves some of the advantages of sequential storage at the cost of extra space and an additional access cycle, is to use an auxiliary vector of locations or pointers: if S (Fig. 2.4(b)) is a one-dimensional structure containing values V_i which are not all of uniform length, an additional vector S* is set up, each of whose elements contains the location of the corresponding element of S. The elements of S* are of uniform length and can be accessed via an index register in the usual way and, having obtained the necessary location, the relevant value V_i can be reached by a second store access cycle. Notice, however, that the time to access any element is still independent of its position in the set.

This method as described has assumed that the length of S_i is fixed when i is given, i.e., that the 'boundaries' within the sequential area S do not change their positions. By extending the auxiliary vector S* to contain the length of S_i as well as its location, this restriction can be removed, but it is then necessary to compare this current length with the length of any new value V_i' presented for storage, and if necessary to relocate the items in store. Unless space is at a premium, relocation downwards (to close gaps) need not be carried out, as the logical ordering is contained in the sequential area S*, not S.

Array storage

Criterion (1) of the characteristics leading to a simple sequential representation was that the data structure should be one-dimensional, but, perhaps surprisingly, some other structures can be mapped on to a sequential storage structure without too much difficulty. As a natural extension of the vector, consider a two-dimensional array M with p rows and q columns (Fig. 2.5).

If sets of row elements are stored together, row by row, in a sequential area beginning at S, then the element M(i, j) (where $0 \leqslant i \leqslant p - 1$ and $0 \leqslant j \leqslant q - 1$) is represented by the contents of location S + qi + j (in other words, this is the mapping function). To access all the elements of row i, we should therefore calculate and store the value S + qi, and then use this as the base from which to access all elements of the ith row vector in the manner already described; to

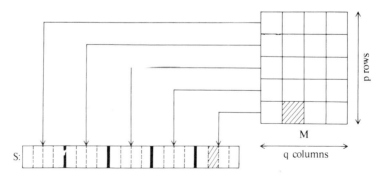

Fig. 2.5   Mapping of a two-dimensional array

access all the elements of the jth column vector, we could use incremental steps of size q, or alternatively, if access 'by rows' was unnecessary or rare, the array could be stored initially with sets of column elements together.

Arrays of more than two dimensions are not easy to visualize, but they occur quite naturally in practice: consider, for example, the braking distance, D, of a moving car: D depends on the speed, V, at the time the brakes are applied, the weight, W, of the car, the coefficient of friction, F, between the tyres and the road, the reaction time, R, of the driver, and other factors too. Mathematically, we can write

$$D = D(V, W, F, R)$$

and the values of D can be recorded as the elements of an array of four dimensions. (When written on paper there would be a set of two-dimensional arrays in which, say, V and W vary, each array corresponding to a fixed pair of values of F and R.) This data structure can be stored in a sequential area S by an extension of the two-dimensional technique, leading to a mapping function of the form

$$D(i, j, k, l) = S + qrsi + rsj + sk + l,$$

where there are p, q, r, s distinct values of V, W, F, R respectively, and the array is stored primarily by order of V, within this by order of W, and so on. (Fig. 2.6 illustrates the case p = 3, r = 4, q = s = 2.)

More generally, the mapping function always has the form

$$D(i, j, k, l) = S + d_1 i + d_2 j + d_3 k + d_4 l,$$

where d_1, d_2, d_3, d_4 are constants depending on the size of the array and the manner in which it is stored.

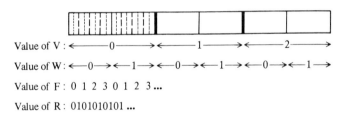

Value of V : ←——0——→ ←——1——→ ←——2——→

Value of W : ←—0—→ ←—1—→ ←—0—→ ←—1—→ ←—0—→ ←—1—→

Value of F : 0 1 2 3 0 1 2 3 ...

Value of R : 0101010101 ...

Fig. 2.6

Access vectors

An alternative approach to the storage of a two-dimensional array is to use an auxiliary 'access vector' or 'Iliffe vector' to indicate the location of a row or column within the array rather as described for variable length data (Fig. 2.4(b)). This eliminates the multiplication necessary when calculating the address for every access, at the cost of the additional storage needed for the access vector, V, and access to any element is correspondingly faster.

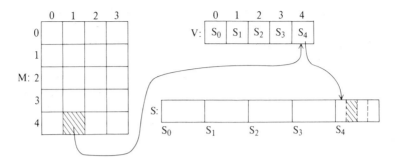

Fig. 2.7 Use of an access vector for a two-dimensional array
$$M(i,j) \rightarrow [V(i), j] \rightarrow S_i + j$$

This method (Fig. 2.7) emphasizes the structure of the array as a set of vectors, and clearly has special merit if operations on the array are localized to a substructure. A common operation which becomes particularly simple is the interchange of two rows, which can be effected merely by switching the corresponding elements in V so that, for example, V(3) contains S_4 and V(4) contains S_3.

Arrays of more than two dimensions can be associated with sets of access vectors; each set corresponds to one dimension of the array and gives the displacement in store for that dimension, so that

$$M(i_1, i_2, \ldots, i_n) \rightarrow [V1(i_1), i_2, \ldots i_n] \rightarrow [V1(i_1), V2_{i_1}(i_2), i_3, \ldots] \rightarrow \ldots$$

The case n = 3 is illustrated in Fig. 2.8.

When access vectors are used, the substructures of an array (the row or column vectors in the case of a two-dimensional array) need no longer be stored consecutively. Furthermore, by reordering the elements of an access vector, the substructures can, if necessary, be rearranged without altering the storage locations of the array elements themselves. This form of array storage therefore has some of the flexibility of the linked storage structures described later in this chapter, while retaining most of the spatial economy and speed of access of a sequential structure.

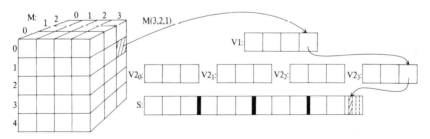

Fig. 2.8 Access vectors for a three-dimensional array

Sparse matrices

An array which has very many zero elements, not regularly distributed, is known as a *sparse matrix*. Such matrices occur in the solution of some network and engineering problems, and are usually very large, so that it may be impracticable to store all their elements. The problem can be reduced to manageable size if it is possible to store only the non-zero elements, which typically form less than 20% of the total.

One method is to store sequentially the non-zero value of an element and also its coordinates in the array. Access to an element is then somewhat similar to the use of an ordered directory: an estimate is made of the likely position of the element in the sequential area, the coordinates at this point compared with those required, and an adjustment made according to the result of the comparison. Alternatively, the non-zero elements can be located with the help of a bit map; this contains 0 or 1 for each zero or non-zero element respectively, and the number of 1's preceding a coordinate position corresponds to the location of that element within the sequential area.

Unfortunately the zero's of a sparse matrix, besides being randomly distributed, are frequently changed in number and position by operations on the matrix, so that additions and deletions must be made in the representation. As already stated (see Fig. 2.3), this causes problems for any form of sequential storage structure, and hence sparse matrices are more commonly represented by linked storage structures, though such methods require more space (for storing the explicit links) and more time (to follow the links). This is the recurring conflict between convenience and economy.

Other sequential representations

To illustrate other mapping functions, we will consider two specialized data structures which can be conveniently mapped on to a sequential area.

A 'band matrix of width three' is a two-dimensional square array all of whose elements have the value zero except for those on the leading diagonal and on the diagonals adjacent to this (see Fig. 2.9(a), in which a cross represents a value which in general is non-zero). Such a matrix is an important feature of the numerical solution of many partial differential equations, and it will be observed that, of the n^2 elements in an n x n matrix, only $3n - 2$ at most are non-zero. Thus a method which stores only the elements in the band permits very great economy in storage requirements compared with the general method, provided the structure can be represented efficiently. If the non-zero elements are stored sequentially by rows, with the first element at location A, then element $M(i, j)$ is stored at location

$$A + 2i + j \qquad (0 \leqslant i, j < n; \; |\,i - j\,| \leqslant 1).$$

Obviously this mapping function is easily calculated.

Band matrices of width five and more also occur, but the technique cannot be extended. When the band width exceeds three, the initial and final rows must be

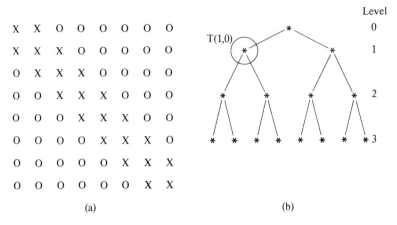

Fig. 2.9 (a) Band or tridiagonal matrix
(b) Balanced binary tree

treated as special cases, and no single mapping function is possible. Band matrices of any width, and also triangular arrays, can however be conveniently represented by using access vectors as described previously in this chapter.

Figure 2.9(b) represents a 'balanced binary tree', i.e. a tree structure in which every element except those at the lowest level has exactly two successors, and thus there is a complete set of elements at each level. We can describe an element by its level and its position within that level, reading from top to bottom and from left to right, and counting from zero as for the array; the element $T(1, 0)$ is marked as an illustration. This structure may be stored sequentially, starting at location $(S + 1)$, by using the mapping function

$$T(i, j) = S + 2^i + j, \qquad (0 \leqslant i < n, \quad 0 \leqslant j < 2^i),$$

and once again this function is easily calculated in a binary computer.

A random path of left and right choices through the structure must necessarily involve accessing each subroot in turn by use of the mapping function. However a path such as 'choose all lefthand elements starting from subroot $T(p, q)$' can be followed more easily: obtain the displacement of the subroot from S, i.e., $2^p + q$, then repeatedly double this value until the lowest level is reached; this gives the displacements of all the subordinate lefthand elements. For example, in Fig. 2.9(b), the element $T(1, 0)$ is stored at location $S + 2$ and its lefthand subordinates are stored at $S + 4$ and $S + 8$. To obtain the righthand subordinates, add one after doubling but otherwise proceed as before: from $T(1, 0)$ we should reach locations $S + 5$ and $S + 11$.

If a binary tree is not strictly balanced, it may nevertheless be worthwhile to obtain the speed and simplicity of a sequential storage structure by writing in zero or null values. A rather similar problem occurs when storing a sparse matrix: in each case there is a break-even point at which the space used in

26

storing uninformative zero values must be weighed against the ease of access to a sequential structure. However, this point is reached from opposite directions: in the case of an array, as we have seen already, sequential storage is the norm, and we consider whether to abandon it when representing a sparse matrix; for tree structures, whose configuration is fluid, sequential storage would be economical but is in general too inflexible to be adopted, and links within the data structure must be represented explicitly.

Linked storage structures

In a sequential storage structure, every element has a natural successor, namely the element occupying the next unit of store (where a 'unit' may be one byte, one word, or a multiple word), and this natural succession is taken to represent the data structure subject to certain over-riding checks to prevent the succession being carried too far. This simple representation breaks down when an element has a successor which, although well-defined at any moment, is not predictable in advance. The situation is similar to a manual telephone exchange, in which the incoming call may require connection to any one of a set of subscribers; the solution is also similar: a flexible connection or link which can be 'plugged into' the appropriate socket without altering the position of the elements being connected.

In practice, there is not one but a *set* of elements, each of which may be linked to some other member of the set (as any subscriber may be linked to any other). Figure 2.10(a) represents the situation as it would appear in the physical store, with the elements in fixed positions and a skein of links; Fig. 2.10(b) shows the logical relationships more clearly without reference to the physical storage.

This figure shows a particularly straightforward case, since every element has at most one successor. More complex structures, in which an element may have more than one successor, can of course occur (cf. Fig. 1.9) but the simple linear list of Fig. 2.10 is sufficient to introduce the principles of using explicit links to provide a flexible representation of a data structure.

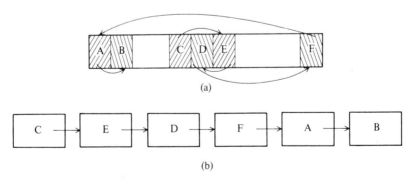

(a)

(b)

Fig. 2.10

27

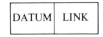

| DATUM | LINK |

Fig. 2.11

Each element of the storage structure now has basically the format shown in Fig. 2.11. DATUM and LINK are called fields of the element: LINK contains the address of the (unique) successor of the element, while DATUM contains a coded representation of the non-structural data associated with the data item. (In practice there may be not one but several DATUM fields of type 'string', 'integer', etc., but one will be taken as typical.) To refer to one of the fields we write, e.g., LINK(ELEMENT), thus selecting one aspect of the element for attention; note the analogy with the mathematical notation $f(x)$, which indicates the generation or calculation of some function dependent on the basic variable x.

For any one class of elements, the format is normally fixed, so that access functions to the individual fields can be simply defined; however, a structure may well contain more than one class of elements. Frequently (and in Algol W, see chapter 3) the LINK field is restricted to refer to elements of a stated class or classes; this is done to avoid programming errors (which are otherwise difficult to detect) in which a LINK leads to an element of the wrong class and, as a result, to the use of an inappropriate field. (Consider, for example, two classes of element having fields of the same length, but with the first containing a 'string' DATUM and the second an 'integer' DATUM.)

Initial and final links
Besides the inner connections of the linear list shown in Fig. 2.10, it may be necessary to refer to the list as a whole, and we therefore require an additional link or 'reference' variable START, whose value is the position of the first element of the list (Fig. 2.12). This reference variable has the same characteristics as the LINK fields of the set of elements to which it refers, and in particular it is just as liable to change. However, the *location* in which the initial reference is held is fixed, as this is associated with the name 'START' (or whatever name is used) at the time that the user's program is assembled or compiled. For the variable START, as for any element of the linear list, it is important to distinguish the location or area of store to be used (which is fixed) from the contents of that location or area (which will almost certainly vary).

Figure 2.12 also shows that there must be some indication of where the storage structure ends; without this it would be possible to access the LINK field of every element in turn and, after reaching the element with value B, to repeat

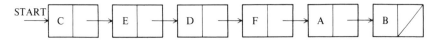

Fig. 2.12

the process and access some undefined and quite irrelevant area of store. It must be remembered that, because of the structural flexibility of a list, the programmer is unlikely to know *ab initio* whether a particular element is the final member of the structure. Hence some special value should be stored in the link field of the final element which is (a) easily tested by the programmer and (b) leads to a system error if the programmer attempts to treat it as a normal pointer. This special value is normally referred to as NULL, and represented diagrammatically by a diagonal line as in Fig. 2.12.

Use of a temporary or 'travelling' pointer

A structure, by its very nature, involves a number of autonomous items and reference may be necessary to any one of these. When the structure is fixed, and stored in a sequential area, it is sufficient to know the leading position and the mapping function in order to refer to any element by its displacement from that position. However, when the storage structure uses explicit links, there may be no single 'leading position' (consider the representation of a digraph), and even when such an element exists (as in the linear list of Fig. 2.12) reference to any general element via this position involves following a linked chain of arbitrary length. For this reason the processing of linked storage structures makes much use of 'reference variables' or 'pointers' to refer directly to a particular element without traversing a lengthy set of links.

Such variables have the same form as the START pointer mentioned in the previous section: they occupy fixed locations, but the contents of a location are interpreted as the address of some point in the store and may be changed at will to point to different elements of the structure.

To illustrate the use of reference variables and their interaction with the LINK fields of a structure, consider again the linear list of Fig. 2.12, and suppose that it is required to print the DATUM field of each element in the list (but the number of elements which the list contains is not known to the programmer). The START pointer must not be disturbed during the execution of this routine if we wish to retain access to the list as a whole for further processing; therefore, to refer to a general element, some other reference variable, TEMP, must be introduced, which marks the position we have reached. This is illustrated in Fig. 2.13 and the routine is shown overleaf. It is written in Algol W, a programming language which will be described more fully in chapter 3, but the comments which are incorporated should make the interpretation straightforward.

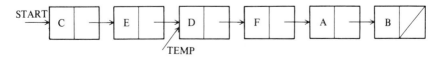

Fig. 2.13   General position while printing DATUM fields of a linear list

```
COMMENT          Routine to print the DATUM fields of a linear list;
TEMP := START;
COMMENT          TEMP initially points to first element. Now enter
        loop, testing for a NULL pointer value on each entry. When
        found continue execution from CONT;
WHILE TEMP ¬ = NULL DO
BEGIN WRITE (DATUM (TEMP));
        COMMENT    Print current DATUM field;
        TEMP := LINK(TEMP);
        COMMENT    Use current LINK field to move on, then
        re-enter loop;
    END;
CONT:
```

The operations which can be carried out on storage structures will be discussed more fully in later chapters; for the moment we consider other natural data structures and the creation of suitable representations for them.

Stacks, queues, and deques

Recall that these three data structures are linear lists in which additions and deletions occur only at the ends of the list while the 'internal' elements, if any, remain unchanged. In this chapter, the argument has been put forward that a sequential storage structure offers economies in space and processing time, but that explicit links are necessary to represent a flexible data structure adequately: in which category should these restricted linear lists be placed?

If we use a sequential area of store we can reserve a vector V of length N, say, and associate with it two index registers I1, I2 (see Fig. 2.14); these registers will contain values which indicate the current ends of the linear list which is being represented (I1 alone would be sufficient for a stack) and a typical operation to add a value X to a stack would be:

```
If I1 = N THEN GOTO OVFLO;
COMMENT exit to OVFLO when vector is fully used;
I1 := I1 + 1;
V(I1) := X;
```

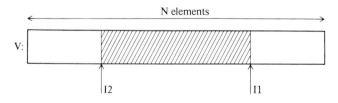

Fig. 2.14

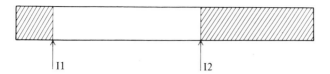

Fig. 2.15

One problem is immediately obvious – how large should N be? These special lists all occur when certain operations or actions arise in an unpredictable order and have to be 'remembered' until there is a suitable opportunity to carry them out. In some cases it is possible to state an upper bound for N, but this is likely to be vastly in excess of the actual maximum in all but the most rare and pathological situations: to 'trace' a tree structure possessing K elements could entail remembering K – 1 elements on a stack, but a more probable maximum is log K. Thus we may choose a realistic value for N, the vector size, on a probabilistic basis but, if so, we must also provide a separate method of handling the rare exceptions which overflow the assigned space (even if the method does no more than report the error).

Figure 2.14 suggests a further difficulty, namely that I1 may reach its upper limit while I2 indicates that space is still available at the lower end of the storage vector. This problem does not apply to the sequential representation of a stack, for which only I1 changes, but is particularly acute for a queue whose elements must, by the nature of the addition and deletion operations on them, inevitably occupy positions steadily further to the right hand (upper) end of the area. A 'wrap-around' storage algorithm can be adopted (Fig. 2.15) in which, once the top of the sequential area has been reached, an attempt is made to re-use locations which have been released at the bottom of the area, but of course the vector will again become fully used if I1 'catches up' with I2.

The only solution to the overflow problem is to reallocate the available sequential space, moving the elements of the list to new locations. If the problem involves a number of special lists stored in consecutive vectors V_1, V_2, V_3, . . ., then the relative sizes of these areas may be adjusted wihout increasing the overall demand for space. Space reorganization can be a time-consuming process, and these problems show that a sequential storage structure is not ideally suitable for representing a special linear list; although structural changes occur only at the ends of such a list, its maximum size is unpredictable and so is the relative activity at its two ends (except for a stack).

Other representations of linear structures
Besides links which are essential to represent connections inherent in natural structures, storage structures may also contain further links which are introduced to aid the *processing* of the representation. Suppose that a finite set of objects is used or examined in strict rotation: for instance, an internal mail

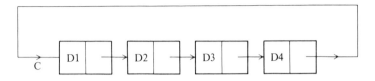

Fig. 2.16   Representation of a circular list, C.

service visiting departments in turn, or the stages of an automated process. It may then be convenient to set up a circular list as shown in Fig. 2.16.

This is still regarded, somewhat paradoxically, as a linear structure, because it contains no branch to any other structure; in fact the only new feature is that the successor of the 'last' element is defined, not as NULL, but as the first element of the list.

Another special representation is a *double-linked* or *two-way* linear list, in which the predecessor and the successor of each element are explicitly indicated (see Fig. 2.17). Of course any element P (other than the first element) of any linear list has a predecessor because, by definition, the element P is the successor of some element Q, and Q is unique because the list is linear; hence Q is the predecessor of P. However, in a single-linked list the predecessor of an element P is not indicated and has to be *found* by examining each element from the beginning of the list to discover whether P is its successor. A double-linked representation simplifies this process, and is used whenever a linear structure is equally relevant in either direction (e.g., an airline route). We shall see later that this representation is of particular value when additions and deletions are necessary in the middle of a linear list.

The first and last elements of a linear list have no natural predecessor and successor, respectively, but it is sometimes convenient to regard them as linked to each other; we then obtain a double-linked circular list which has the characteristics of both types of representation.

Representation of trees and digraphs

Trees and digraphs are structures which embody many interrelationships between their elements and whose form is frequently subject to change. Thus, except in very specialized cases such as a balanced binary tree (Fig. 2.9), the only appropriate representations are those which use explicit links; not only are the structures very flexible, but any given element may have more than one successor. Furthermore, in the case of a digraph, where 'rings' may occur, it is not always possible to order all the elements.

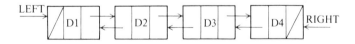

Fig. 2.17   A two-way representation of a linear list

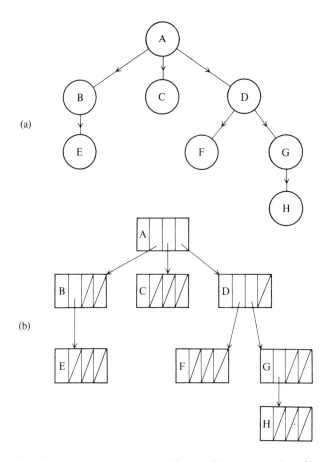

Fig. 2.18 (a) A tree structure; (b) a possible representation of it

Explicit links represent the structural aspects of data well, as illustrated for a tree in Fig. 2.18, but a difficulty arises when an item of data may possess an arbitrary number of successors. In most high-level programming languages the format of an element which represents an item of data must be specified in advance: how many link fields should be allowed for? It is, of course, possible to set a maximum size, but this implies an arbitrary restriction on the representation and, at the other extreme, leads to a considerable waste of storage space when few links are required. Even at assembly-code level, it is clear that the necessary length of each element must be known to permit correct access to its fields.

When this length may change dynamically, the only alternative to an arbitrary upper limit is to structure the element itself — that is, to represent each item of data by its own list instead of by a unified element; each element of the list represents some aspect of the item. Fig. 2.19 shows the same tree structure as

33

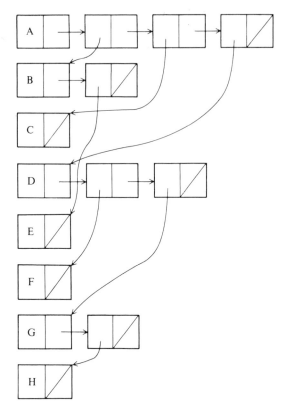

Fig. 2.19 Alternative 'structured' representation of the tree shown in Fig. 2.18 (a)

before when represented in this way, and Fig. 2.20 applies the technique to a digraph. It is clear that storage space is required for the extra links introduced by this method of representation, but no elements contain unnecessary space; the balance of advantage between the methods illustrated in Figs. 2.18–20 depends on the degree of structural uniformity exhibited by the given data – if all items have approximately the same number of connections, the former method is the simpler.

If DATUM and LINK fields require comparable amounts of store, a *pointer* to a terminal element (e.g. C, E, F, H, W) can be replaced by the *value* of such an element, and the terminal representation itself dispensed with. Corresponding to Fig. 2.18, we now have Fig. 2.21. The disadvantage of this method is that it becomes necessary to mark and test each field (other than the first), to determine whether it represents a link or the value of a terminal element which is replacing a link. The apparent saving in space is thus reduced by the space for markers; similarly, the time taken to process a marker must be set against the ability to detect a terminal element without examining all its fields.

34

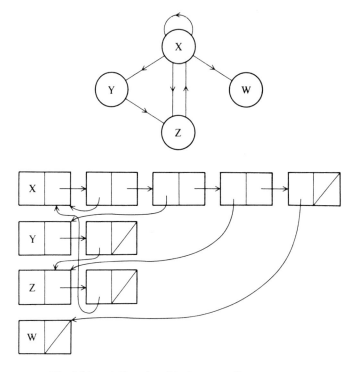

Fig. 2.20   A digraph and its 'structured' representation

In Figs. 2.19 and 2.20, it will be noticed that the name or value of a data item always occurs in the representation as the first field of the first element reached by a 'left' pointer. This means that there is no problem in distinguishing values from links, but to reach *all* the values could be a lengthy process. An alternative representation is illustrated in Fig. 2.22: one list links all the values of the structure together and associates each value with a list in which the corresponding structural relationships of that item are represented. The 'structure list' of a value has one element for each link which can be followed

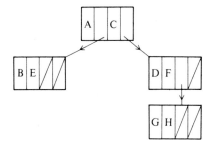

Fig. 2.21

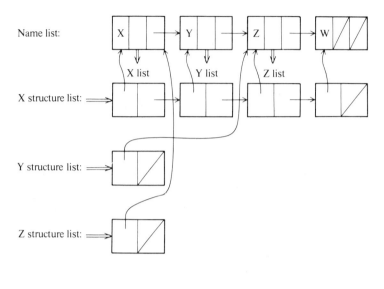

Name list:

X list   Y list   Z list

X structure list:

Y structure list:

Z structure list:

W structure list: NULL

Fig. 2.22   Alternative representation of the digraph shown in Fig. 2.20

from the data item in question (thus there is no structure list for W); links are represented by pointers to the appropriate element of the 'name list', from which further paths can be followed if relevant. By this means the links and the values of a data structure can be separated in any problem in which only one of these aspects is of interest. The additional storage requirements amount to only one field per value as compared with the method of Fig. 2.20.

Binary trees

Remember that a 'tree' was defined in chapter 1 (p. 12) as containing at least one element, the root, with the remaining elements, if any, forming disjoint subsets, each of which is itself a tree.

A 'binary tree' is an important structure which, as its name implies, has the general form of a tree but which is restricted to at most two branches at every root or subroot. More precisely, there are two commonly used definitions:

Definition 2.1 *A strict binary tree* contains a root alone or contains a root and two ordered disjoint subsets each of which is itself a strict binary tree.

An alternative and more convenient definition used by Knuth (1973) is:

Definition 2.2 *A general binary tree* is either empty or contains a root and two ordered disjoint subsets each of which is itself a general binary tree.

These definitions are confusingly similar but should be carefully distinguished (Fig. 2.23 may help). A strict binary tree must be non-empty and regular

36

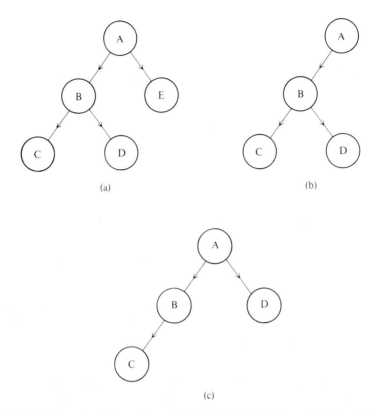

Fig. 2.23 Examples of binary trees; all satisfy Definition 2.2, but only (a) satisfies Definition 2.1

(though not symmetrical) in the sense that every left subtree implies the existence of a right subtree and vice versa. By contrast a general binary tree can be empty and, by applying this property to any subtree, does not require symmetry at a subroot. (Note that a single branch will still be designated 'left' or 'right' as appropriate, because binary trees are ordered.)

These definitions imply that every strict binary tree is also a general binary tree, but not conversely, and that a general binary tree is a special case of a tree if and only if it is non-empty. Henceforth if the term 'binary tree' is used without qualification, this will refer to the less stringent case of a general binary tree. A major application of binary trees (of either type) is their use in the representation of more general structures.

Representation of a tree as a binary tree

If a general tree structure can be mapped onto either of these binary structures, the storage representation can take advantage of the regularity of the elements of binary trees, which involve just three fields — left link, datum, and right link.

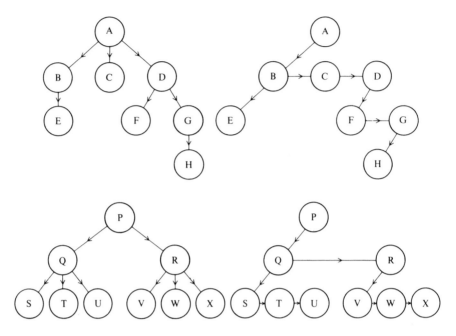

Fig. 2.24   Two examples of the 'natural representation' of a tree as a general binary tree

The simplest mapping, which uses a general binary tree (Definition 2.2), is sometimes called the 'natural representation' of a tree as a binary tree. The transformation is

1 keep every link from an element of the tree to its eldest son;
2 link each element to its next oldest brother, if any (i.e., link all the direct successors of an element);
3 delete all other links of the tree structure.

Fig. 2.24 shows two examples of this mapping, the first being the tree structure previously considered in Figs. 2.18, 2.19, and 2.21. The resulting binary trees may look unusual, but a more familiar appearance can be achieved by redrawing the horizontal links in a downward pointing direction (or by tilting the page clockwise through 45°).

In a mapping which uses a strict binary tree (Definition 2.1), the crucial idea is that each *link* of the tree is replaced by a *node* in the strict binary tree, while each node of the tree becomes a leaf (a terminal node) of the strict binary tree. The transformation is

1 at each node of the tree (starting at the root) consider the links from left to right, and represent each link by a binary node;
2 the left binary subtree represents the subtree of the link;
3 the right binary subtree represents the remainder of the tree, i.e. the right

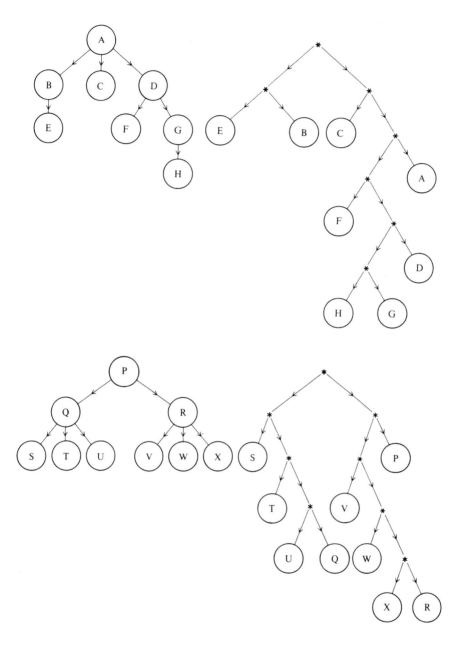

Fig. 2.25   Two examples of trees represented by strict binary trees

son is a binary node which represents either the 'next' link from the root of the tree (see (1)) if such a link exists, or the root itself.

This 'symmetric' mapping is illustrated in Fig. 2.25, using the same trees as in Fig. 2.24. An asterisk indicates a root which has two link fields but no datum field.

Notice that the natural representation introduces no new nodes, but involves a substantial number of NULL links; the symmetric representation requires more elements but these divide into two classes – either terminal (datum field only), or branch (exactly two link fields). Thus the space requirements of the two mappings are almost identical.

Maintenance of a source of available storage space for linked structures

A linked storage structure in general develops unpredictably, and at any point in the structure a new element may be required or an existing element may become redundant. As a result, not only do the links of the structure look like a tangled skein, but also the unused area of store becomes fragmented and intermingled with elements of the storage structure.

This situation leads to two problems:

1 how to keep track of 'free' store;
2 what action to take when an element in use becomes redundant

Any discussion of linked storage structures must indicate how these can be solved.

The first problem is reasonably straightforward; the free store can be considered as a set of unused elements, and these are all linked together initially to form a linear list; when space is required to represent a new element, one such area is claimed from this 'free list'. If the storage structure involves only one class of element, a single free list is sufficient; if several classes are involved and are of different sizes, it may be necessary to create a free list to cater for each size of element.

The second problem is not as simple, chiefly because it is difficult in a complex structure to recognise *when* an element becomes redundant. The whole question of free-store maintenance will be considered in more detail in chapter 5, when basic operations on structures have been discussed.

Summary

This chapter has considered methods of *creating storage structures* to represent the naturally occurring data structures of chapter 1. The method of storage chosen depends critically on the ways in which the data are to be interrogated, the frequency with which this occurs, and the number and type of the modifications which may be made. For static structures, space can be allocated in sequential areas and advantage taken of access functions which depend on parameters defining the (predictable) position of an element. Such access is fast, and little or no space is required for data links.

For dynamic structures, explicit links must be used to obtain sufficient flexibility of representation, but any given structure can be mapped into store in a number of ways. In some cases it is convenient to introduce additional links, besides those which are essential to represent the structure, to simplify processing of the information. Dynamic changes in structures fragment the available storage space, and hence this too must in general use explicit links, in conjunction with a suitable method of tidying up space which is released from use.

Problems

2.1 What are the important factors which influence the choice of a suitable model or method of representation for a data structure?

2.2 Discuss some possible methods of representing the structure and content of musical notation in a form suitable for computer storage. Consider, for example,

(a) single notes in the scale of C major
(b) the duration of notes
(c) notes where a sharp or flat is to be played
(d) chords
(e) key signatures
(f) rests.

2.3 A *lower triangular* matrix, T, is such that $T(i,j) = 0$ when $i < j$, where $0 \leqslant i, j < n$. What is the mapping function which will allow this matrix to be stored, row by row, in a vector V which has $\frac{1}{2}n(n + 1)$ elements?

What is the corresponding function for an upper triangular matrix, for which $T(i,j) = 0$ when $i > j$?

2.4 Write down a mapping function which will allow the non-zero elements of an $n \times n$ band matrix B of width 5 to be stored in a two-dimensional array A with 5 rows, each row representing one 'diagonal' of B.

2.5 The non-zero elements of a two-dimensional sparse matrix S may be represented by the columns of another two-dimensional array A such that, in any column of A, the first two rows are the coordinates of a non-zero element of S and the third row is the value of the element. For example

$$S = \begin{pmatrix} 0 & 0 & 0 & 1 \\ 0 & 4 & 0 & 0 \\ 0 & 0 & 0 & 0 \\ 0 & 0 & 3 & 0 \\ 0 & 2 & 7 & 0 \end{pmatrix} \rightarrow A = \begin{pmatrix} 1 & 2 & 4 & 5 & 5 \\ 4 & 2 & 3 & 2 & 3 \\ 1 & 4 & 3 & 2 & 7 \end{pmatrix}.$$

The columns of A may be ordered by the row coordinates of S (as shown) or by the column coordinates. How could the array A be extended to allow straightforward access to the elements of S in either row or column order?

If S is a p x q matrix with k non-zero elements, for what values of k does A use less storage space than S in each case? (Assume that row and column coordinates occupy the same amount of space as elements of S.)

2.6 Design a suitable storage allocation for each of the following arrays and give algorithms for accessing elements from each array.

(a)   The non-zero elements only of the array

$$A[1:10, -10:10],$$

where

$$A_{ij} \neq 0 \quad \text{if } |j| \leqslant i$$
$$= 0 \quad \text{otherwise.}$$

(b)   The array consists of rows of strings of characters each of variable length.

(c)   A skew-symmetric array $A[0:100, 0:100]$ (i.e. $A_{ij} = -A_{ji}$ if $i \neq j$) using minimum storage.

(Queen Mary College, London, 1974)

2.7 A *complete* binary tree is one with all levels filled, except possibly the last, and this last level is filled from the leftmost position. Show that it is possible to implement a complete binary tree without using pointers (links).

Give an Algol W procedure (or a corresponding algorithm) to traverse a tree implemented in such a way, in the order left—root—right, printing the values. You may assume that the values are integer numbers, and that the number of nodes in the tree is contained in a global integer variable *size*.

(Glasgow, 1974)

2.8 In a tree structure, it is necessary

(a)   to locate a sub-root whose value is given
(b)   to print all values subordinate to a given sub-root value
(c)   to find the predecessor of a given value.

Discuss the most suitable forms of representation in each case. Would any of your choices be altered if the tree were known to be a binary tree?

2.9 If a linear list has relatively few internal changes, it may be represented as a *compact list* (Hansen) in which elements occupy successive sequential locations unless an explicit link indicates otherwise. For example the list of Fig. 2.10 might appear as

where an asterisk indicates that the cell is to be treated as a link.

Give algorithms to add or delete a member of a compact list at a point indicated by specifying the element of the list just previous to the one to be inserted or removed. You may assume that sublists are not used by more than one main list.

What difficulties are enountered when two lists *may* share a common sublist?

(St Andrews, 1973)

3. Algol W – a general-purpose high-level language applicable to structures

Once we have decided on the form of a storage structure which will represent some naturally occurring problem, there remains the question of how to implement it: that is to say, how to describe its construction and specify operations on it. To some extent we had in mind the characteristics of a computer store in choosing the storage structure, but at that stage we did not consider such details as the amount of store needed to represent a link, or how to describe the format of an element, or what basic operations we needed to transform a structure. These details must now be settled, and to describe them precisely we require a notation or language.

At the assembly-language level, there are a number of statements and directives which enable the user to reserve areas of store, define constants, and carry out logical or arithmetic operations on binary patterns, whatever those patterns may represent. These provide the essential 'building blocks', but we are seeking a notation more closely associated with the structural aspects of the data, in which it is possible to refer to blocks of store which may vary dynamically in their size, content, and interrelationship.

One solution is to write macro-statements which combine (or can be expanded into) a set of assembly-language statements giving the required structural operations. This means that the user is still essentially programming at assembly-language level, but his program is shorter to write and reflects more clearly the specialized operations he is using. However, low-level languages, by their nature, tend to be machine dependent and therefore restricted in their availability, besides being tedious if used for large-scale problems.

High-level languages overcome these difficulties, but in general impose restrictions on the data formats and statements which can be used. Storage structures take such general and variable forms that it is almost impossible to devise complete language facilities for all applications, and recent languages such as Algol 68 make provision for the user to define his own data types and operations on them.

Even fixed data structures such as arrays received scant attention in early high-level languages. When using Fortran, the size of an array must be stated at compile time, even if this means that the space claimed is much greater than necessary once the run-time parameters are known. Algol 60 allows 'dynamic' arrays, but provides no array operators; thus to scalar multiply the vectors v1, v2, each having n elements, we must write

s := 0;
for i := 1 step 1 until n do s := s + v1(i) * v2(i);

compare this with APL, in which it would be sufficient to write

s ← + /v1 × v2

Algol W could be described as a halfway house between Algol 60 and Algol 68; it does not have the flexibility and generality of Algol 68, but it includes virtually all the features of Algol 60 together with some valuable additions — notably, provision for operations on strings, for the definition of data elements containing 'fields' of several different types, and for the introduction and manipulation of links to these elements, thus creating a linked storage structure. It is therefore a language which can be used to describe operations on structures such as those introduced in chapter 2, and which is easily learnt by anyone with experience of Algol 60. Readers with experience in other high-level languages such as Fortran will require more practice, but should not find the examples difficult to follow.

Basic features of Algol W

An Algol W program has the same structure as a program written in Algol 60, and consists of a 'block' which contains 'declarations' of 'identifiers' chosen by the user, followed by 'statements' in which these identifiers are used in conjunction with constants and 'basic symbols'. An identifier in Algol W may be a single letter, or a letter followed by a sequence of letters and digits up to 256 characters in length (Algol W uses the IBM System 360 EBCDIC alphabet and all letters are upper case).

A simple program can consist of just one block, but a block — regarded as a set of instructions — can itself act as a statement and hence any one block can have others nested within it. The limits of a block are indicated by the basic symbols BEGIN and END, and Algol W makes no distinction between a block in which declarations occur and one which contains only a set of statements.

Two typical Algol W programs are shown in Figs. 3.1 and 3.2. They demonstrate the traditional 'Algol format', but have also been chosen to illustrate minor points of difference between Algol 60 and Algol W; some comments on the examples are given below. A more comprehensive description of the language differences is given in Appendix 1. In this chapter, we shall consider in detail only those facilities of Algol W that do not exist in Algol 60 — the handling of strings and record structures.

Commentary on the examples

(The line numbers are for reference only and are not part of the Algol W programs.)

```
BEGIN COMMENT THIS PROGRAM WILL READ AND SUM SETS OF POSITIVE INTEGERS
      PUNCHED ON CARDS SUCH THAT EACH SET ENDS WITH 0 AND THE END OF ALL
      DATA IS INDICATED BY –1. FOR EACH SET THE PROGRAM WILL PRINT THE
      SIZE OF THE SET AND THE SUM OF ITS MEMBERS;

      INTEGER N, SIZE, TOTAL;
      READ(N);
REPEAT: SIZE := TOTAL := 0;
      WHILE N¬ = 0 DO
      BEGIN SIZE := SIZE + 1;
            TOTAL := TOTAL + N;
            READON(N)
      END;

      COMMENT END OF ONE SET REACHED. PRINT SIZE AND TOTAL, THEN TEST FOR
            END OF ALL DATA;
      WRITE ("SUM OF", SIZE, "INTEGERS IS", TOTAL);
      READON(N);
      IF N¬ = –1 THEN GOTO REPEAT
END.
```

Fig. 3.1

Figure 3.1

Line

1–4 After COMMENT all symbols up to a semicolon will be ignored during program execution.

6 READ is a built-in standard procedure. It commences reading on a new card, and may have any number of parameters.

7 REPEAT is a label identifier defined as such by the following colon. No other declaration is required.

8–12 The WHILE statement replaces the WHILE element of Algol 60. The loop is re-entered so long as the logical expression remains true, then control goes to the next statement (line 15). The loop in this example is a block. Note the symbol for 'not equal'.

11 READON is similar to READ, but continues from a previous position on a card, moving to the next card only if all values have been read.

15 WRITE (and WRITEON) give output on the lineprinter and correspond in operation to READ/READON. The print list may contain simple variables (e.g., SIZE), expressions (e.g., M/N in Fig. 3.2, line 14), or constants. Character-string constants are enclosed in double quotes and printed exactly as typed.

18 The final END of a program must be followed by a full stop.

Figure 3.2

Line

7 Q is a dynamic array, with upper bound defined at run time, hence a new block is required following the READ statement in line 6.

7 The word REAL must be stated and is not optional as in Algol 60.

46

```
BEGIN COMMENT THIS PROGRAM WILL READ A SET OF N NUMBERS PUNCHED ON CARDS
         AND STORE THEM IN AN ARRAY Q THEN CALCULATE THEIR MEAN.
         THE FIRST ITEM OF DATA MUST BE THE VALUE OF N;

     INTEGER N;
     REAL M;
     READ(N);

     BEGIN REAL ARRAY Q(1 : : N);
         M := 0;
         FOR I := 1 UNTIL N DO
             BEGIN
             READON(Q(I));
             M := M+Q(I)
             END;
         WRITE ("MEAN OF", N, "NUMBERS IS", M/N)
     END
END.
```

Typical input:

        6

        12.2   5.9   −4.3   27.0   −6.9   8.4

Output:

        MEAN OF   6 NUMBERS IS 7.0500000

Fig. 3.2

7   Note that bound pairs are separated by double colon, and that
    parentheses are used in all references to arrays (see also lines 11,12)

9   I is an INTEGER control variable of the FOR statement and need
    not be declared. Its scope is restricted to the FOR statement. The
    increment and limits must be integer expressions and are fixed on
    entry to the FOR statement.

9   STEP ⟨increment⟩ can be omitted when the increment is 1

10–13 The object of the FOR statement is a block (not containing further
       declarations). I is valid for the duration of this block.

Distinctive features of Algol W

String handling

A string was defined in chapter 1 as an ordered set of characters from some
alphabet. To distinguish between an identifier which represents some value, and
a string of characters, the latter is enclosed in double quotes when input to, or
used in, an Algol W program. For example,

    ABC4 is an identifier (provided it appears in a declaration applicable to the
            block in which it is used)
    "ABC4" is a character-string constant
    "12X" is a character-string constant
    12X has no meaning in Algol W.

47

Character-string constants can occur in WRITE statements (see Figs. 3.1, 3.2), but a string variable must be used if an output statement will vary the characters printed. For example, it may be necessary to print the name of each department when making financial returns: in this case, we wish to store the name of each department and use a variable which can be assigned each name in turn.

Characters are stored in their binary-coded (EBCDIC) form, and, since each EBCDIC code has 8 bits, up to 4 characters can be stored in one 32-bit word. Obviously many strings, such as names or addresses, are longer than this and hence the declaration of a string identifier must specify the number of characters which this variable will represent (up to a maximum of 256). Typical string declarations are

> STRING (6)   GROUP;
> STRING (10)   FIRSTNAME, SURNAME, NAME;

Once a string identifier has been declared, it can be given a value by either a READ statement or a string assignment statement such as

> SURNAME := "ROBINSON";
> NAME := SURNAME;

The characters of the righthand string are assigned simultaneously to the corresponding positions on the left and if the string on the left of the assignment is the longer, space characters are assigned to its extra positions. The length of the string being assigned must not exceed the length of the string on the left. In the above example, NAME and SURNAME both acquire the value

> "ROBINSON ⊔⊔"

where ⊔ indicates a space character.

When a value is obtained from a READ statement the same rules apply, except that the string to be assigned must be punched on a card and enclosed in double quotes.

Some programs refer to a set of related character strings, such as a set of departmental codes. The concept of an array is extended to cover this case, and the program includes a *string array declaration:* for example,

> STRING(4) ARRAY DEPTCODE (1::15);

which reserves space for 15 strings each of length 4.

Substrings

It is often necessary to select one or more characters from within a longer string. For this purpose the positions in a string are associated with the numbers 0,1,2, . . . starting from the left and the operator ' | ' is used to select a substring of the required length starting at a specified position. For example,

> NAME (0 | 3) selects the substring "ROB" of length 3
> NAME (5 | 5) selects "SON ⊔ ⊔" of length 5.

More generally a 'substring designator' is

⟨string variable⟩ (⟨integer expression⟩ | ⟨integer number⟩),

the ⟨integer expression⟩ giving the starting position and ⟨integer number⟩ the length (which must exceed zero). Clearly the sum of the position number and the length must not exceed the length of the initial string.

Example

Some lines of text have been punched on cards, followed by the character '∗'. Read the cards, count the number of times that a particular substring of three distinct characters occurs in the text, replace each occurrence by a stated alternative of the same length, and print the result. Figure 3.3 shows the program.

```
BEGIN STRING(80) TEXT;
    STRING(3) OLD, NEW;
    INTEGER TOTAL;
    READ (OLD, NEW);        COMMENT READ STRING TO BE FOUND AND REPLACEMENT;
    TOTAL:=0;
NEXT: READCARD (TEXT);       COMMENT READCARD READS 80 CHARACTER VALUES;
    FOR K:=0 UNTIL 79 DO
    BEGIN IF TEXT(K|1)="∗" THEN GOTO FINISH;
          IF (K<=77) AND (TEXT(K|3)=OLD) THEN BEGIN TEXT (K|3):=NEW;
                                                    TOTAL:=TOTAL+1
                                              END
    END;
    WRITE (TEXT);
    GOTO NEXT;
FINISH:WRITE (TEXT);
    WRITE(OLD, " HAS BEEN REPLACED BY ", NEW, TOTAL, "TIMES")
END.
```

Fig. 3.3

Records and references

Suppose that we wish to store details of a class of students including name, year of study (1,2,3, . . .), a 3-letter code for the course of study, and an average mark to date. This mixture of integer, real, and string values cannot be stored in an array but can be associated by declaring a 'record class' in an Algol W program. Thus the class STUDENT is:

RECORD STUDENT (STRING(15) NAME; INTEGER YEAR; STRING(3) COURSE; REAL MARK);

This declaration does not create or reserve space for members of the record class but defines explicitly the format which each will have. To refer to a member of the record class one must declare a 'reference' variable to act as a pointer in the store, thus:

REFERENCE (STUDENT) JAMES, JOYCE;

Notice that the declaration must state the class of records to which the variables will refer. We can then create 'instances' of the class by the assignment statements

> JAMES := STUDENT;
> JOYCE := STUDENT ("ROBINSON ⎵ JK", 2, "MCS", 62.4);

The former statement creates an instance in which the value of each field is undefined; the latter sets up a record with all its field values defined. (All or none of the values must be defined.) Any aspect or field of a record can be discussed by using the notation

> FIELD (RECORD)

for example,

> YEAR(JAMES) := 3;
> WRITE(NAME(JOYCE),MARK(JOYCE));

If a large number of records are to be created with a common format, a reference array can first be declared: for example,

> REFERENCE(STUDENT)ARRAY MEMBER (1:50);
> FOR I := 1 UNTIL 50 DO MEMBER (I) := STUDENT

and we can then refer to any field of any member of the set, e.g., to read the name of the first member

> READ (NAME (MEMBER(1)));

The fields of a RECORD must be 'simple variables', and hence arrays and nested records are excluded. However a REFERENCE variable is a simple variable and may therefore occur as a field within a record. This is an extremely important feature, since it means that a field within one record can point to another record, thus linking the records together whatever their position in store. We will re-define the record class STUDENT to include such a field;

> RECORD STUDENT(STRING(15) NAME;INTEGER YEAR;
> STRING(3)COURSE; REAL MARK;
> REFERENCE (STUDENT)LINK);

Then we may link in the store the records of two students who are following the same course:

> IF COURSE(JAMES) = COURSE (JOYCE) THEN LINK(JAMES) :=
> JOYCE

If the course codes do not agree, then LINK(JAMES) could be left undefined, but this would not show that a test had been made, and it is better to indicate this positively. To do so the special reference value NULL can be assigned:

> LINK(JAMES) := IF COURSE(JAMES) = COURSE(JOYCE)
> THEN JOYCE ELSE NULL;

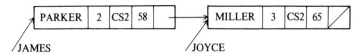

Fig. 3.4   Simple use of record structures

The storage which has been set up is a simple linear list of the form presented diagrammatically in Fig. 3.4.

More complex structures can be created by having more than one reference field within a record, leading possibly to different 'classes' of records. For example (Fig. 3.5) students may be associated with departments as a result of defining two record classes:

RECORD STUDENT(STRING(15) NAME; INTEGER YEAR;
        STRING(3) COURSE; REAL MARK; REFERENCE(DEPT)MAIN;
        REFERENCE(STUDENT)LINK);
RECORD DEPT (STRING(10) DNAME; STRING(10) FACULTY);

Sometimes it is possible for a reference to be made to alternative classes of record: some students taking a course may be 'extra mural' students sponsored by a company rather than a department. We should then have a third class of record, COMPANY, and the reference variable MAIN within student records may be associated with either this class or DEPT. Typical declarations would be

RECORD STUDENT (...; REFERENCE (DEPT,COMPANY)MAIN;
        REFERENCE (STUDENT)LINK);
RECORD COMPANY (STRING(12) CNAME;STRING(50) ADDRESS);

If a value has been assigned to MAIN for a particular student JAMES, it is possible to test which class of record this refers to by using the predicate IS, which yields the value TRUE or FALSE; e.g., to print company addresses for extramural students:

IF MAIN (JAMES) IS COMPANY THEN
    BEGIN P := MAIN(JAMES);
        WRITE(CNAME(P), ADDRESS(P));
    END;

Further examples of the use of records will occur in the following chapters.

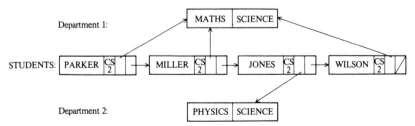

Fig. 3.5   Chain of students taking a common course but based on different departments

51

Problems

The following exercises are not essential for an understanding of the remainder of the book but are provided for students who wish to have some practice in using Algol W, particularly if they have access to facilities for testing their solutions. Some of the problems may be solved either as self-contained programs or as general-purpose procedures. Problems 3.1–3 use programming features which are not restricted to Algol W, problems 3.4–7 involve string handling, and problems 3.8–10 concern record classes.

3.1 You are given as data a set of integers, all of which are less than 100. The size of the set is not known, but it is followed by the special number 100. Count the number of zero values contained in the set and the number of negative values, and calculate the average of all the positive values. Print your results with suitable captions.

3.2 A company's employees are required to pay a pension contribution which is 6 per cent of their salaries. After this, the first £1000 of net salary is tax free, the next £3000 is taxed at 30 per cent, and each subsequent £2000 is subject to a further 10 per cent tax up to a maximum of 70 per cent on any net income exceeding £10 000. Given a set of salaries punched on cards, print a table showing gross salary, pension contribution, tax, and salary payable in each case.

3.3 Read a set of 16 positive integers into an array, sort them into ascending order, and print them.

3.4 A set of eight 8-character names are punched on a card with two spaces between each. Use READCARD to place them in a buffer of length 80 characters. Sort the names and print them in alphabetical order.

   (A method similar to that in Problem 3.3 may be used, since character strings are compared character by character on the basis of their EBCDIC codes (Fig. 2.2) until the first unequal characters are found. Thus

   "A" < "B", "BE" < "BET", "BAT" < "BEG", "BAY" < "BEE".

If the strings are unequal in length, the shorter string is treated as having spurious additional space 'characters' so that "BE" = "BE ⌴ ".)

3.5 The mailing list of a firm consists of a file of punched cards containing entries ordered by surname, e.g.,

   JONES, A.B., 4 ABBEY ROAD, ST ANNES, BARCHESTER.

The prefix 'MRS.' or 'MISS' is recorded before the initial when appropriate.

   Write a program that will read a card and print its contents as they should appear on an address label.

3.6 The name of a country and of its capital city are punched on a card. Read a set of such data and print it in tabular form, centred under the headings 'Country' and 'Capital' respectively. For example:

```
   COUNTRY          CAPITAL
   *******          *******
   FRANCE            PARIS
   BELGIUM          BRUSSELS
    SPAIN            MADRID
UNITED STATES      WASHINGTON
```

3.7 A passage of text has been punched on cards and is left-justified except at new paragraphs (i.e., aligned at the left margin). Write a program that will read the text line by line, adjust the inter-word spacing to make the text right-justified also, and print the result.

3.8 A personnel file is to contain an employee's name, age, sex, date of appointment, and salary. Read from cards sets of data of this type and store each set in a record which is accessed by an element of a reference array; the first item of data to be read is the number of employees in the firm. Find and print

(a) the average salary of all employees;
(b) the number of employees receiving salaries which are above the average for the firm as a whole;
(c) the number of women employees and their average salary;
(d) the name of the longest-serving employee.

3.9 Students from five different departments are attending a course and the class list contains the name of each student and the department on which he is based. Declare a reference array with five elements to correspond to the departments, read the class list into records each having two fields NAME and LINK, and attach each new record to the front of its appropriate set. When all the data have been read, print out lists of the students from each department.

3.10 The transport department of a large firm is based at a central depot, and distributes goods to customers throughout the country. As each lorry leaves the depot, its fleet number and destination are punched on a card, and when it returns, its fleet number and the number of the bay where it is parked are punched on a second card. Each set of cards is sorted into order of fleet number at the end of each day.
Write a program that will

(a) read the data from each set of sorted cards and create two sets of linked records with suitable formats;

(b)   merge these two sets into a single list arranged in order of fleet number, deleting any lorries which occur in both the outward and the inward sets, so as to obtain a list of vehicles whose 'status' has changed since the previous day;

(c)   print out the list of changes, giving the number of each vehicle involved and either its destination or its location in the depot, whichever is appropriate.

4. Basic operations on storage structures

Sequentially stored stacks and queues

Having introduced the programming language Algol W, we can reconsider in a more precise way some of the storage structures described in chapter 2.

Although sequential storage is not, in general, suitable for variable structures, it can be used, as suggested on pp. 30, 31, for stacks and queues. The method requires two pointers to define the sequential area in use, and in writing algorithms for the stack and queue operations, it is most important to consider the situations which occur when the structure is almost full or empty. Suppose (to be precise) that integer numbers are to be stored and that a sequential area of N locations is thought to be sufficient. Then the declarations can be

    INTEGER ARRAY BLOCK(1::N);
    INTEGER F,L;

The variables F(first) and L(last) will act as pointers to the stack or queue (Fig. 4.1) and in the initial (empty) state we may take $F - L = 0$.

For a stack L alone is sufficient and the algorithms are as follows:

S1: to add a value V to a stack.

    IF L = N THEN GOTO OVFLO;
    L := L + 1;
    BLOCK(L) := V;

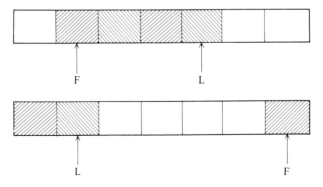

Fig. 4.1 Pointers defining a 'cyclic' sequential queue structure

55

S2: to print and remove a value from a stack:

IF L = O THEN GOTO UNFLO;
WRITE (BLOCK(L));
L := L − 1;

In these algorithms, OVFLO and UNFLO are error routines which are accessed if an attempt is made to overfill or underfill the stack.

The algorithms for a queue use the sequential area in a cyclic manner, and hence adjacent values of F and L may indicate either a fully used queue or one which is almost empty. The initial value F = L = 0 is reset if and only if the queue is emptied, in order to distinguish the results of these two cases:

Q1: to add a value V to the end (L) of a queue:
IF L = N THEN L := 0;
L := L + 1;
IF L = F THEN GOTO OVFLO;
BLOCK(L) := V;
IF F = 0 THEN F := 1;
Q2: to print and remove a value from the front (F) of a queue:
IF F = 0 THEN GOTO UNFLO;
WRITE (BLOCK(F));
IF F = L THEN F := L := O ELSE BEGIN IF F = N THEN F := 0;
F := F + 1
END;

Multiple stacks and queues

END;

If the available sequential area must be shared between several stacks and/or queues, it is necessary to delimit both the area *available* to each structure and also the area currently *used* by each structure; this requires an additional 'top of area' pointer T for each structure (Fig. 4.2), but the algorithms stated above can then be applied to the ith structure, subject to the following simple amendments:

F   must be replaced by F_i
L   must be replaced by L_i
N   must be replaced by T_i
0(zero) must be replaced by T_{i-1} if $i > 1$.

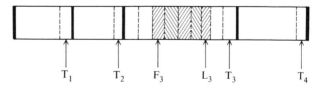

$$T_1 \qquad T_2 \quad F_3 \qquad L_3 \; T_3 \qquad\qquad T_4$$

Fig. 4.2

(Notice that if there are k structures in all, then $T_k = N$. To avoid stating a special case for the first structure, it may also be convenient to define a value $T_0 \equiv 0$.)

The error exits remain as before, but there is one very important difference in their meaning: whereas UNFLO still indicates a terminal state, an overflow condition can now occur in one structure while free space still exists in the sequential area as a whole. In this case a relocation of the structures can permit operations to be resumed.

The principles used in the method of relocation may be very simple or quite sophisticated. At one extreme, the algorithm may look only for the nearest stack or queue which is not using all its allotted space, and move the intervening elements by the one space necessary to rescue the overflowing structure. This is a rapid solution, but overflow is liable to recur immediately. At the other extreme, the algorithm can take account of the way in which each structure is changing and, when overflow occurs, reallocate the sequential area so as to give the most free space to those structures which have grown most rapidly since the last reallocation. There is, of course, no guarantee that this growth will continue, but no better guide is available. An algorithm of this type has been described by Garwick and by Knuth (see exercise 4.4).

Content of the structures

The above discussion has for simplicity spoken of 'one space' per element, but any other uniform number of spaces may be used merely by incrementing or decrementing the pointers by an appropriate value. Similarly, the integer numbers used as an example can be replaced by logical values, strings of characters, real numbers, etc. if a suitable array declaration is made initially; e.g., to represent elements containing up to four characters each the declaration would be

STRING (4) ARRAY BLOCK (1 :: N);

Linked linear storage structures

When each element of a structure is linked explicitly to its successor or successors (rather than implicitly by sequential position), the representation is much more flexible, and when structural changes occur it is sufficient to alter pointers without the need to relocate the elements themselves to maintain the ordering. The price to be paid for this simplification is, of course, the space required to store the explicit pointers, and the time required to access an element by following a chain of links.

In order to consider algorithms for the addition and deletion of elements in linked linear structures, we must first set up a suitable structure. We make the following declarations, which will be assumed to be valid throughout this chapter:

RECORD ELEMENT (STRING(1) DATUM; REFERENCE (ELEMENT)LINK);
REFERENCE (ELEMENT)FIRST, LAST, T, T1;

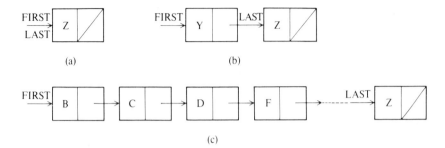

Fig. 4.3 Three stages in the construction of a typical linear list

The former defines the format of the list elements and, since it would be impossible to refer to any members of the record class without an initial pointer, the latter defines some necessary pointer variables.

A typical member of the class can now be created (Fig. 4.3(a)) by the statement

LAST := FIRST := ELEMENT("Z", NULL);

The character "Z" has no particular significance, but we wish to ensure that the LINK field of the element has the value NULL, and Algol W insists that all or none of the field values are specified when a record is created.

To create a second record and link it to the first (Fig. 4.3(b)) it is sufficient to make the statement:

FIRST := ELEMENT("Y", FIRST);

and a series of such statements will establish the linear list of consonants shown in Fig. 4.3(c).

Stack operations

In general, addition at the front (FIRST) end of a list can be achieved by the statement used immediately above when creating the list. Printing and deletion at the same end requires the statements

WRITE(DATUM(FIRST));
FIRST := LINK (FIRST);

However, these must be amplified to cater for the extreme situations. In a linked storage structure, 'overflow' occurs only when all available storage has been used, and we shall discuss later the maintenance of a pool of free space, but on the other hand an empty stack must be recognized when attempting to delete elements. If the stack contains only the datum "Z", then the value of FIRST after the deletion operations is NULL; hence we take FIRST = NULL initially, and the stack algorithms become:

S3: to add a value "V" to a stack:
T := ELEMENT ("V",FIRST);
IF FIRST = NULL THEN FIRST := LAST := T ELSE FIRST := T;

S4: to print and delete a value from a stack:
IF FIRST = NULL THEN GOTO UNFLO;
WRITE (DATUM(FIRST));
FIRST := LINK (FIRST);

Queue operations
Elements are added to the queue at the rear (LAST) end of the list and deleted at the front. Hence the deletion algorithm is exactly the same as for a stack. The addition algorithm is:

Q3: to add a value "V" to a queue:
T := ELEMENT ("V",NULL);
IF FIRST = NULL THEN FIRST := LAST := T
        ELSE BEGIN LINK (LAST) := T;
                LAST := LINK (LAST)
        END;

Notice that in queue operations the initial value of LAST can be undefined, as an empty queue is adequately defined by the condition FIRST = NULL.

Internal list operations
If the position where an element is to be added or deleted is neither the front nor the rear of a list, a 'travelling pointer' must be introduced to search the list and locate the required position by its DATUM field (say "D"); while doing this, care must be taken to look out for the end of the list, in case the desired element is missing.

T := FIRST;
WHILE (LINK(T) ¬ = NULL) AND (DATUM(LINK(T))(¬ = "D") DO
                              T := LINK(T);
IF LINK(T) ¬ = NULL THEN WRITE (DATUM(LINK(T)));

When this step is complete, the pointer T is standing at the element *preceding* the one where addition or deletion is to take place (i.e. at "C" in Fig. 4.4) and, as a check, the DATUM field of the successor element has been printed. T is moved no further because the link to "D" must now be broken and attached instead to a new element (if addition is to take place) or to "F" (deleting "D").

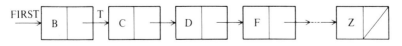

Fig. 4.4

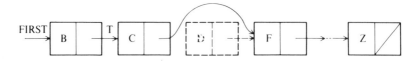

Fig. 4.5

In the latter case (Fig. 4.5), the statement is

LINK(T) := LINK(LINK(T));

Note that "D" itself is still attached to "F", but this is of no interest since the former element can no longer be accessed.

The careful reader will observe that a flaw will appear in this algorithm if the list is initially empty and FIRST = NULL. This can be remedied, and some of the statements made less cumbersome, by using a second travelling pointer T1 which always moves one step ahead of T. The deletion algorithm becomes:

```
T1 := FIRST;
WHILE (T1 ¬= NULL) AND (DATUM(TI) ¬= "D") DO
            BEGIN T := T1;
                      T1 := LINK (T1)
            END;
IF T1 = NULL THEN WRITE ("ELEMENT MISSING")
            ELSE  BEGIN WRITE (DATUM(T1));
                            IF T1 = FIRST THEN FIRST := LINK (T1)
                                          ELSE LINK(T) := LINK (T1)
            END;
```

The use of a travelling pointer is a very common device in linked data structures, and fills much the same role as an access or address formula in a sequential structure: the unpredictable nature of a linked structure precludes the generation of a direct reference to a particular element, and instead it is necessary to travel along a chain of links to reach any element.

Two-way linked lists

A 'trailing pointer' (T trails T1 in the algorithm above) is a common device in a storage structure which uses one-way links and where internal changes occur; however, it is unnecessary if two-way links are introduced (see Fig. 2.17, p. 32) to permit immediate access to both neighbours of any given element.

Consider a symmetrical record format defined by

```
RECORD SYMELT (REFERENCE(SYMELT) LLINK;
            STRING(1)DATUM; REFERENCE(SYMELT) RLINK);
REFERENCE(SYMELT) LEFT, RIGHT, P;
```

60

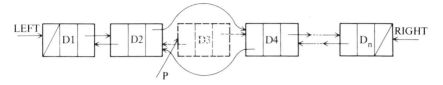

Fig. 4.6   Two-way list after an element has been deleted

The basic operations needed to print and delete the element indicated by P (Fig. 4.6) are:

    WRITE(DATUM(P));
    RLINK(LLINK(P)) := RLINK(P);
    LLINK(RLINK(P)) := LLINK(P);

but, once again, provision must be made for limiting cases and then the algorithm becomes:

    IF P = NULL THEN BEGIN WRITE("NON-EXISTENT ELEMENT");
                              GOTO ERROR
                  END;
    WRITE(DATUM(P));
    IF LLINK(P) = NULL THEN LEFT := RLINK(P)
                        ELSE RLINK(LLINK(P)) := RLINK(P);
    IF RLINK(P) = NULL THEN RIGHT := LLINK(P)
                        ELSE LLINK(RLINK(P)) := LLINK(P);

Observe the perfectly symmetrical nature of the deletion algorithms for a two-way list and the absence of any auxiliary pointers. The problem of adding a value at a stated point in the list can be solved in a very similar manner (see Exercise 4.8). Unfortunately, the ease of programming with double-linked lists must be bought at the cost of the space required for an extra reference field in every element.

Ring structures
A compromise between the spatial demands of two-way lists and the convenience of being able to access any element from any other can be achieved by using a circular list (Fig. 2.16). In order to orientate the otherwise perfect symmetry of a ring it is often desirable to have a distinctive format for a 'list-head' or 'ring-start' element which can contain information relevant to the ring as a whole, such as a group name or code number, the time of last amendment, or the number of elements in the ring. The ring-starts may themselves be linked in a ring to form a structure well suited to the representation of subgroups or components, as suggested in Fig. 4.7 (where the

61

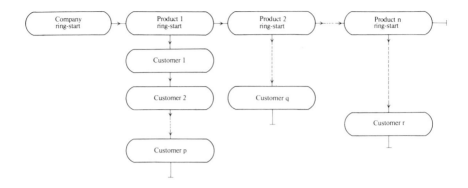

Fig. 4.7   Typical ring structure

symbol ⊣ indicates a pointer which returns to the head of its list to create a ring).

As a simple illustration of operations on such a structure, suppose that it refers to a rental company which maintains records of its most recent customers in unordered circular lists (from which entries are later transferred to ordered files). Each ring concerns a different type of equipment rented by the company and elements on the ring contain the name and address of each customer, the date of his rental agreement, and the serial number of the item supplied. In addition, the ring-start element contains the type-name for its ring, the number of customer records in the ring, and the number of circuits made of the ring – as a measure of its activity. New entries are added after the ring-start element, but access to existing entries is made by customer name, with the search beginning at the arbitrary point where the previous enquiry was completed.

The following procedure, given a customer's name as the value of ENQUIRY, prints the contents of the customer's record (or reports that the search has failed) and, if necessary, updates the ring-start element. Customer records belong to the class

    RECORD CUSTOMER (STRING(15) NAME; STRING(50) ADDRESS;
        INTEGER DATE, SERIALNO;
        REFERENCE (CUSTOMER,STOCK)LINK);

and ring-start elements belong to the class

    RECORD STOCK(STRING(10)TYPE; INTEGER TOTAL, FREQUENCY;
        REFERENCE (CUSTOMER,STOCK)LIST);

(Notice the use of the predicate IS in the procedure to distinguish the ring-start from customer records.)

62

```
PROCEDURE OUTPUT(STRING(15) VALUE ENQUIRY);
BEGIN REFERENCE(CUSTOMER, STOCK)Q;
    Q := P;   COMMENT P STANDS AT PREVIOUS ENQUIRY
        RECORD;
    IF Q IS STOCK THEN Q := P := LIST(P);
    WHILE NAME(P) ¬= ENQUIRY AND LINK(P) ¬= Q DO
        BEGIN
        P := LINK(P);
        IF P IS STOCK THEN
            BEGIN FREQUENCY(P) := FREQUENCY(P) + 1;
                P := LIST(P);
                IF P = Q THEN GOTO EXIT
            END
        END;
EXIT: IF NAME(P) = ENQUIRY THEN
            WRITE(NAME(P), ADDRESS(P), DATE(P), SERIALNO(P))
        ELSE WRITE("NO RECORD FOUND FOR", ENQUIRY)
END OUTPUT;
```

Operations on tree structures

Operations on a tree structure must necessarily involve accessing some or all of its elements, and since a 'follow your nose' philosophy is not sufficient for traversing non-linear structures, the first crucial requirement is a systematic method of traversal which will 'visit' every element of the tree once and once only. Given such an algorithm, it is possible to carry out an operation related to any specified element, whether this is to compare, delete, add, print, or take any other action.

Just as the irregular number of branches causes problems in designing a storage structure for a general tree, so it makes it difficult to describe a traversal algorithm concisely. Since there are at least two ways in which a general tree can be mapped on to a binary form, a traversal of a binary tree structure can also help to provide a solution to the more general problem.

Traversal of a binary tree

The most common methods of traversal reflect the recursive nature of a general binary tree.

One algorithm, known as *preorder traversal*, emphasizes the structural importance of a root. It is as follows:

visit the root of a binary tree,
then visit the left subtree of the root and traverse it in preorder,
then visit the right subtree of the root and traverse it in preorder.

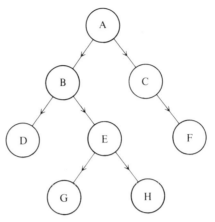

Fig. 4.8   A general binary tree

When applied to the binary tree shown in Fig. 4.8, preorder traversal would visit the elements in the order ABDEGHCF.

Alternatively, a more symmetric route may be taken, known as *postorder, inorder,* or *symmetric traversal,* for which the rules are:

> visit the left subtree of the binary root and traverse it in symmetric order, then visit the root,
> then visit the right subtree and traverse it in symmetric order.

Figure 4.8 in symmetric order is DBGEHACF. (In this book, the word 'symmetric' will be used for this method of traversal; the term 'postorder' has unfortunately been used also in a contradictory sense to describe the traversal of a binary tree in the order left subtree, right subtree, root.)

Traversal of a general tree structure

To apply these traversal rules to a general tree one must first use one of the transformations which map the tree on to a binary tree. Taking the trees shown in Figs. 2.24 and 2.25 (pp. 38, 39) as examples, we obtain the following orders for a tree which is represented as a general binary tree:

Preorder	Symmetric order
ABECDFGH	EBCFHGDA
PQSTURVWX	STUQVWXRP

When a tree is represented as a strict binary tree, preorder and symmetric order are identical (since the roots of the strict binary representation contain no data values). For the same examples, either order of traversal is

EBCFHGDA
STUQVWXRP.

Notice that the latter orders are the same as those obtained by traversing the general binary representation symmetrically, and thus adoption of this order of traversal has the merit of being independent of the type of binary mapping which is used to represent the tree. In terms of the original tree structure, the rules for symmetric traversal are:

visit the leftmost subtree and traverse it in symmetric order,
then visit the remaining subtrees (if any) from left to right
    and traverse each one in symmetric order,
finally visit the root of the tree.

Numerous other algorithms have been suggested for traversing a tree structure (Knuth (1973); Page and Wilson (1973)), and one which arises in a particularly natural way when a tree is considered in its original form is known as 'levelorder'. In this method, each element at a given level or depth in the tree is visited, then traversal moves to a new level. Working from the root downwards, the trees of Figs. 2.24 and 2.25 in levelorder are, respectively,

ABCDEFGH
PQRSTUVWX.

If the tree is transformed and represented as a binary tree (of either kind) then elements formerly at level d are found by taking d left links in the binary tree, interspersed with 0, 1, 2, ... right links. The first few elements at level d in the original tree can now be described in the following way (not all of these routes will exist):

$$l_1 \; l_2 \cdots l_d$$
$$l_1 \; l_2 \cdots l_d r_1$$
$$\cdots$$
$$l_1 \; l_2 \ldots l_d r_1 \; r_2 \cdots r_q$$
$$l_1 \; l_2 \cdots l_{d-1} \; r_1 \; l_d$$
$$\cdots$$
$$l_1 \; l_2 \cdots l_{d-1} r_1 \; l_d \; r_2 \cdots r_q$$
$$l_1 \; l_2 \cdots l_{d-1} r_1 \; r_2 l_d \; r_3 \cdots r_q, \text{etc.}$$

Tree structures as data

A traversal algorithm visits every element of a tree once and once only and enables any operation on the elements to be carried out unambiguously, but the result of the traversal conceals the structure of the tree: for example, the binary trees in Fig. 4.9 are quite distinct in structure, but symmetric traversal gives the same result in each case.

By contrast, if a tree structure forms the data for some problem, and must be read into store, it is essential that the data describe the relationships of the elements as well as their values. Fortunately, the fact that a root may have any number of branches, and hence the description of a subtree is of arbitrary length, causes no problems in an input operation, because the description does not change, whereas the storage structure created from the description is likely to be altered by subsequent operations on it.

A simple notation which adequately describes tree-structured data is a version of the Dewey classification system used in many libraries. This assigns to each element a number corresponding to its seniority in every subtree of which it is a member, e.g. the third son of the fourth son of the head of the family would be assigned 143. Referring again to Fig. 2.24, the trees can be described in Dewey notation as

1 A	11 B	12 C	13 D	111 E	131 F	132 G	1321 H	
1 P	11 Q	12 R	111 S	112 T	113 U	121 V	122 W	123 X

The number assigned to each element is unique and enables the elements to be stated in any order, but the natural ordering of Dewey notation shown above corresponds to levelorder traversal.

An alternative notation, using brackets in place of numbers, is similar to the parentheses notation used for lists on p. 9, and can be defined recursively as

root (first subtree, second subtree, . . . nth subtree).

The same trees as before, written in parentheses notation, are

A(B(E),C,D(F,G(H)))
P(Q(S,T,U),R(V,W,X))

The former notation is the easier to amend if the data should change for any reason, but the latter is the more concise and associates the elements of each subtree more closely.

Examples of tree-structure algorithms*

Example 4.1 *Construction of a binary tree.* A binary tree is given as data in the parentheses notation described in the previous section, and is to be stored in elements whose format is defined by the record class SYMELT (see p. 60). The procedure FORMBINARY, which reads the data into an 80-character buffer B, is entered recursively to form the binary storage structure. The data is terminated by the character ";", which is read only when the tree is empty, or contains a single root element, or if the data is stated erroneously. In the last case, control is sent to a global label ERROR.

The procedure uses a stack for workspace whose elements belong to the record class

RECORD SYMSTACK(REFERENCE(SYMELT) BRANCH;
REFERENCE(SYMSTACK) CHAIN);

---

*These may be omitted at first reading.

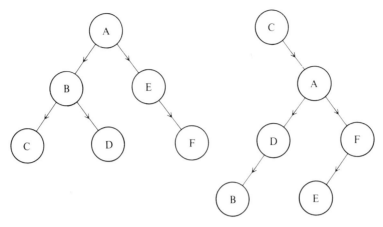

Fig. 4.9   Symmetric order for both these binary trees is CBDAEF

and the integer I indicates the current position in the input buffer B, while the logical variable LEFT shows whether the next element to be read belongs to a left or right branch. The reference variable T is given the value NULL before entering the procedure for the first level of recursion, and after the final exit it points to the completed tree. The flowchart is shown in Fig. 4.10.

```
PROCEDURE FORMBINARY(REFERENCE(SYMELT) T;
        REFERENCE(SYMSTACK) VALUE P;
            STRING(80) B; INTEGER I; LOGICAL LEFT);
COMMENT FOR THE FIRST CALL OF THE PROCEDURE SET
        T = P = NULL, I = 0, LEFT = TRUE;
BEGIN REFERENCE(SYMELT) Z;
        STRING(1) S;
NEWCARD:IF I = 0 THEN READCARD(B);
        S := B(I ⏐ 1);
        IF S = "␣" THEN BEGIN I := (I + 1) REM 80;   COMMENT
                                IGNORE SPACES IN DATA;
                            GOTO NEWCARD
                    END;
        WRITEON(S); COMMENT ECHO DATA AS READ;
        IF S = ";" THEN IF P = NULL THEN GOTO DONE
                ELSE BEGIN WRITE("EXCESS ( IN DATA");
                            GOTO ERROR
                    END;
        IF S = "(" THEN BEGIN LEFT := TRUE; COMMENT LEFT
                                BRANCH AHEAD.KEEP ROOT;
                            P := SYMSTACK(T,P);
                            T := NULL
                    END
```

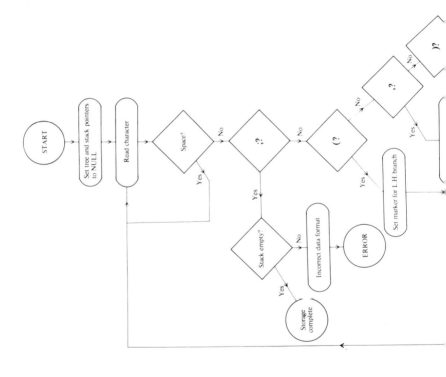

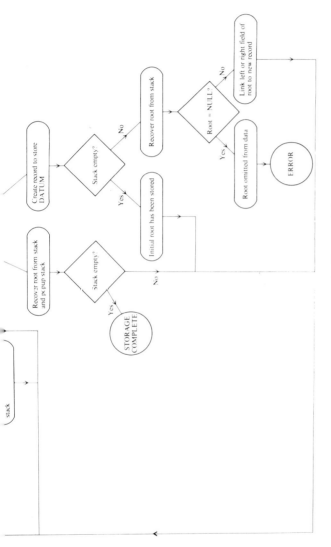

Fig. 4.10   Flowchart for Example 4.1

```
              ELSE IF S = "," THEN BEGIN LEFT := FALSE; COMMENT
                                         RIGHT BRANCH AHEAD;
                                T := NULL
                         END
              ELSE IF S = ")" THEN BEGIN  T := BRANCH(P);
                                          P := CHAIN(P);
                                          COMMENT RIGHT SUB-
                                          BRANCH HAS BEEN
                                          SET UP AND T
                                          RETURNED TO ROOT
                                          POSITION. HENCE
                                          TREE IS COMPLETE
                                          IF STACK IS EMPTY,
                                          ELSE SUBTREE IS
                                          COMPLETE;
                                          IF P = NULL THEN GOTO
                                          DONE
                         END
              ELSE BEGIN COMMENT STORE DATUM. IF STACK IS
                         EMPTY THIS IS ROOT;
                         T := SYMELT(NULL, S, NULL);
                         IF P = NULL THEN GOTO AGAIN;
                         Z := BRANCH(P);
                         IF Z = NULL THEN BEGIN WRITE("ROOT
                                                OMITTED");
                                          GOTO ERROR
                                    END;
                         IF LEFT THEN LLINK(Z) := T ELSE
                         RLINK(Z) := T;
                  END;
       AGAIN:I := (I + 1) REM 80;
             FORMBINARY (T,P,B,I,LEFT);
       DONE:
       END FORMBINARY;
```

Example 4.2 *Symmetric traversal and output of a binary tree.* Given a non-empty binary tree T stored in the form used in Example 4.1, the recursive procedure POSTOUT prints the DATUM field of its nodes in symmetric order.

```
PROCEDURE POSTOUT(REFERENCE(SYMELT) VALUE T);
If T ¬= NULL THEN
BEGIN POSTOUT(LLINK(T));      COMMENT   MOVE TO LEFT SUBTREE;
      WRITEON(DATUM(T));      COMMENT   PRINT ROOT OR LEAF
                                        ELEMENT;
      POSTOUT(RLINK(T));      COMMENT   MOVE TO RIGHT SUBTREE;
END POSTOUT;
```

70

Example 4.3 *Construction of a tree.* A general tree is given in parentheses notation as in Example 4.1, and is to be stored with each element represented in 'structured' form (Fig. 2.19), by means of the recursive procedure FORMTREE.

The value of each element is stored in a record of the class

```
RECORD TNODE(STRING(1)INFO;
     REFERENCE(TELT)STRUCTURE);
```

its branches, if any, are represented by records of the class

```
RECORD TELT(REFERENCE(TNODE)SON;
     REFERENCE(TELT)BROTHER);
```

and the stack used for workspace contains records of the class

```
RECORD TSTACK(REFERENCE(TELT)TBRANCH;
     REFERENCE(TSTACK)TCHAIN);
```

The initial values of the parameters are the same as in Example 4.1 (except for LEFT, which is not required in this case). Figure 4.11 shows the flowchart.

```
PROCEDURE FORMTREE (REFERENCE(TNODE,TELT) T;
     REFERENCE(TSTACK) VALUE P; STRING(80) B;INTEGER I);
BEGIN STRING(1)S;
     REFERENCE(TNODE,TELT) T1;
     T1 := T;
NEWCARD:IF I = 0 THEN READCARD (B);
     S := B(I|1);
     IF S = "␣" THEN BEGIN I := (I+1) REM 80; COMMENT IGNORE
                              SPACES IN DATA;
                         GOTO NEW CARD
               END;

     WRITEON(S); COMMENT ECHO DATA AS READ;
     IF S = ";" THEN IF P = NULL THEN GOTO DONE
                         ELSE BEGIN WRITE("EXCESS ( IN DATA");
                              GOTO ERROR
                              END;

     IF (S = "(") AND (T IS TNODE) THEN
               COMMENT START STRUCTURE LIST OF T;
               T := STRUCTURE(T) := TELT
```

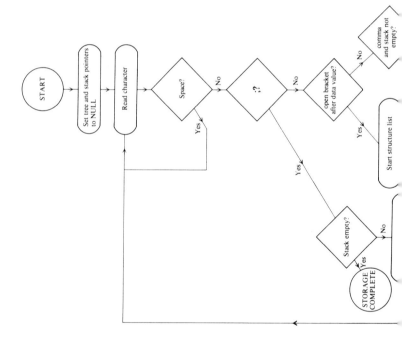

72

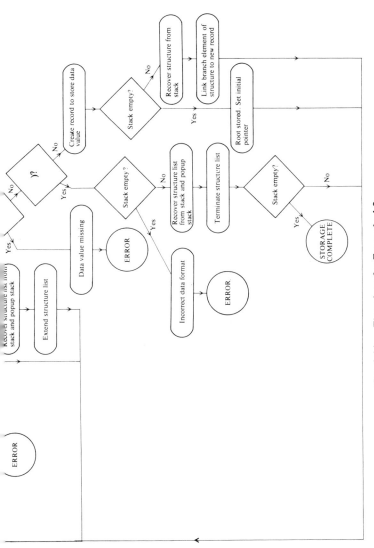

Fig. 4.11 Flowchart for Example 4.3

73

```
        ELSE IF (S = ",") AND (P ¬= NULL) THEN
                BEGIN COMMENT RECOVER STRUCTURE
                    LIST AND EXTEND IT;
                T := TBRANCH(P);
                P := TCHAIN(P);
                T := BROTHER(T) := TELT
            END

        ELSE IF (S = "(") OR (S = ",") THEN
                BEGIN WRITE ("NO DATUM");
                    GOTO ERROR
            END
        ELSE IF S = ")" THEN BEGIN IF P = NULL THEN
                                BEGIN
                                WRITE("DATA ERROR");
                                GOTO ERROR
                            END
                        ELSE COMMENT RECOVER STRUCTURE
                            LIST AND TERMINATE;
                        T := TBRANCH(P);
                        P := TCHAIN(P);
                        BROTHER(T) := NULL;
                        IF P = NULL THEN GOTO DONE
                    END

        ELSE BEGIN COMMENT STORE DATA VALUE. REMEMBER
                BRANCH POINT AND LINK THIS TO DATA
                VALUE EXCEPT AT INITIAL ROOT;
            IF T ¬= NULL THEN P := TSTACK(T,P);
            IF T = NULL THEN T := T1 := TNODE(S,NULL)
                ELSE T := SON(T) := TNODE(S,NULL)
            END;
    I := (I+1) REM 80;
    FORMTREE(T,P,B,I);

DONE:T := T1;
END FORMTREE;
```

Example 4.4 *Transformation of a tree structure to its 'natural representation' as a binary tree.* Given a (general) tree structure, T, in which each element is stored in 'structured' form, the recursive procedure TRANSFORM creates the corresponding natural binary tree S (Fig. 2.24). The reference variable S is given the value NULL before entering the procedure for the first level of recursion, and T is the tree to be transformed; the other initial values and the record classes are as used in Examples 4.1 and 4.3. Figure 4.12 shows the flowchart.

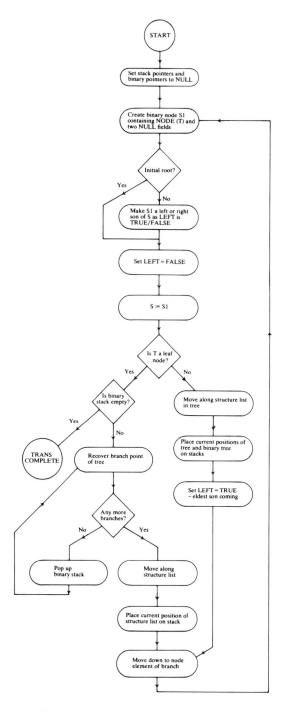

Fig. 4.12   Flowchart for Example 4.4

```
PROCEDURE TRANSFORM (REFERENCE(TNODE,TELT) VALUE T;
    REFERENCE(SYMELT) S; REFERENCE(TSTACK) VALUE PT;
    REFERENCE(SYMSTACK) VALUE PS; LOGICAL LEFT);
BEGIN REFERENCE(SYMELT) S1;

    COMMENT COPY DATA VALUE AND LINK INTO BINARY
        TREE EXCEPT AT ROOT.
        LEFT IS TRUE FOR ELDEST SON OF TREE ROOT,
            OTHERWISE FALSE;

    S1 := SYMELT(NULL,INFO(T),NULL);
    IF S ¬= NULL THEN IF LEFT THEN LLINK(S) := S1 ELSE
        RLINK(S) := S1;

    S := S1;
    LEFT := FALSE;
    IF STRUCTURE(T) = NULL THEN COMMENT T IS LEAF. IF
        BINARY STACK EMPTY THEN TRANSFORMATION
        COMPLETE, OTHERWISE RECOVER BRANCH POINT IN
        TREE;

                        BEGIN NEXT:IF PS = NULL THEN GOTO
                                DONE;

                            T := TBRANCH(PT);
                            PT := TCHAIN(PT);
                            COMMENT IF T IS NULL,
                                NO MORE BRANCHES
                                HERE. RELEASE POINT
                                IN BINARY TREE;
                            IF T = NULL THEN BEGIN
                                    S := BRANCH(PS);
                                    PS := CHAIN(PS);
                                    GOTO NEXT
                                        END

                END

        ELSE BEGIN IF T IS TNODE THEN T := STRUCTURE(T)
                        ELSE T := BROTHER(T);
                COMMENT MOVE TO NEXT BRANCH OF
                    TREE, PREPARE FOR ELDEST SON,
                    KEEP BINARY SUB-ROOT;
                LEFT := TRUE;
                PS := SYMSTACK(S,PS);
            END;
```

COMMENT KEEP TREE SUB-ROOT, THEN RE-ENTER TRANSFORM;
PT := TSTACK(BROTHER(T),PT);
TRANSFORM(SON(T),S,PT,PS,LEFT);

DONE:
END TRANSFORM;

Example 4.5 *Construction of a binary tree using Dewey notation.* The
elements of a binary tree are given in levelorder using Dewey notation and are
separated by commas (e.g., Fig. 4.13(a)). The procedure DEWTOBIN reads the
data into an 80-character buffer B and sets up a binary storage structure
(Fig. 4.13(c)) which is compatible with Example 4.2. The data are terminated
by a semicolon.

During construction of the tree, the Dewey code of an element is stored
temporarily in a separate record and the 'Dewey' records and the 'tree' records
for the current level and the preceding level are linked horizontally as shown in
Fig. 4.13(b).

The reference variable T is given the value NULL before entering the
procedure, and on exit it points to the root of the constructed tree. Provision is
made for a maximum depth of 16 levels. The temporary elements belong to the
record class

RECORD DEWEY (STRING (16) CODE; REFERENCE (SYMELT) ELT);

1 A , 11 B , 12 C , 111 D , 121 E , 122 F , 1111 G , 1112 H , 1222 I ;

(a)

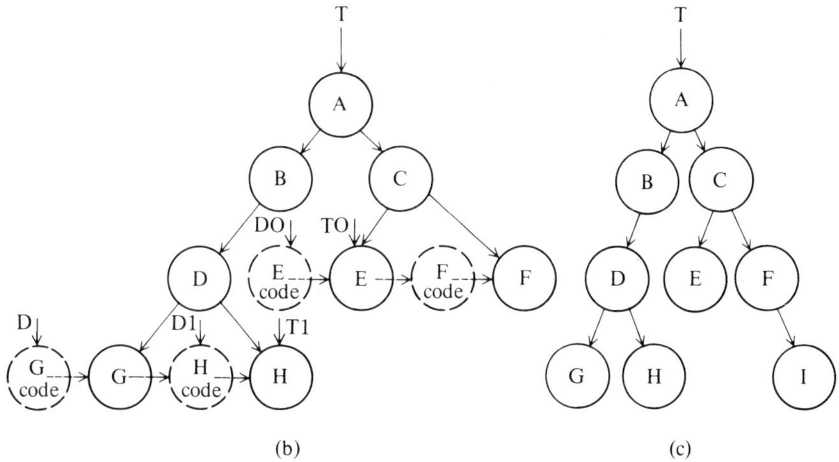

(b)   (c)

Fig. 4.13   (a) Binary tree data in Dewey notation; (b) the corresponding structure at an
intermediate stage (one element still to be added); (c) the completed binary tree structure

and the tree elements belong to the class

> RECORD SYMELT (REFERENCE (SYMELT) LLINK;
> STRING (1) DATUM; REFERENCE (SYMELT, DEWEY) RLINK);

The latter class has the same format as in Examples 4.1, 4.2, and 4.4, but the definition of the RLINK field is extended to allow the temporary introduction of DEWEY elements.

DEWTOBIN uses three subsidiary procedures and its flowchart is shown in Fig. 4.14.

> PROCEDURE DEWTOBIN (REFERENCE(SYMELT)T; LOGICAL U);
>
> COMMENT DEWEY CODES ARE ASSUMED TO BE IN LEVELORDER
> AND TO HAVE AT MOST 16 DIGITS. EACH CODE MUST BE
> FOLLOWED BY A SPACE ON THE SAME CARD. A COMMA
> FOLLOWS EACH DATUM EXCEPT THE LAST, WHERE THE
> END OF DATA IS INDICATED BY A SEMICOLON.
> SET T = NULL INITIALLY, THEN ON EXIT T POINTS TO
> THE COMPLETED TREE PROVIDED U IS TRUE;
>
> BEGIN REFERENCE(SYMELT) T0,T1;
> REFERENCE(DEWEY) D,D0,D1;
> STRING(80)B;
> STRING(16)S;
> INTEGER I,L;
>
> PROCEDURE CLOSE (REFERENCE(SYMELT) TR; REFEERENCE
> (DEWEY) DW);
>
> COMMENT WHEN NEW LEVEL NECESSARY, NULLIFY RLINKS
> OF REMAINING TREE ELEMENTS IN CURRENT LEVEL;
>
> WHILE RLINK(TR) IS DEWEY DO
> BEGIN DW := RLINK(TR);
> RLINK(TR) := NULL;
> TR := ELT(DW)
> END CLOSE;
>
> PROCEDURE NEXTCHAR;
>
> COMMENT FIND NEXT CHARACTER IN DATA, IGNORING
> SPACES;
>
> BEGIN I := (I+1) REM 80;
> IF I = 0 THEN READCARD(B);
> WRITEON(B(I|1));   COMMENT ECHO DATA AS READ;
> IF B(I|1) = "⊔" THEN NEXTCHAR
> END NEXTCHAR;

```
PROCEDURE ERROR (INTEGER N);
    BEGIN WRITE(CASE (N) OF
                    ("CODE NOT FOLLOWED BY SPACE. CODE IS   ",
                    "CODE INCOMPLETE. CODE IS   ",
                    "LEVEL OMITTED. NEW CODE IS   ",
                    "CODE HAS NO PARENT. CODE IS   "));
        S := "⊔";
        FOR J := 0 UNTIL L − 1 DO IF I + J <80 THEN
            S(J|1) := B(I + J|1);
        WRITEON(S);
        IF N = 3 THEN WRITEON(B(I + L|1));
        U := FALSE;
        GOTO EXIT
    END ERROR;

    I := −1;
    NEXTCHAR;
    IF B(I|1) = ";" THEN GOTO EXIT;    COMMENT TREE IS EMPTY;

    COMMENT SET UP ROOT;
    L := 1;
    IF (I = 79) OR (B(I + 1|1) ⌐= "⊔") THEN ERROR(1);

    D := D0 := D1 := DEWEY(B(I|1),NULL);
    NEXTCHAR;
    ELT(D1) := T := T0 := T1 := SYMELT(NULL,B(I|1),NULL);

    NEXTCHAR;
    COMMENT READ SEPARATOR FOLLOWED BY CODE AND
        DATUM TILL SEMICOLON;
    WHILE B(I|1) ⌐= ";" DO
    BEGIN NEXTCHAR;
        IF I + L = 80 THEN ERROR(1);
        IF I + L > 80 THEN ERROR(2);

        IF B(I + L|1) ⌐= "⊔" THEN
        BEGIN COMMENT NEW LEVEL REACHED;
            L := L + 1;
            IF I + L = 80 THEN ERROR (1);
            IF B(I + L|1) ⌐= "⊔" THEN ERROR(3);
            CLOSE(T0,D0);
            D0 := D;
            T0 := ELT(D0);
            D := NULL;
        END;
```

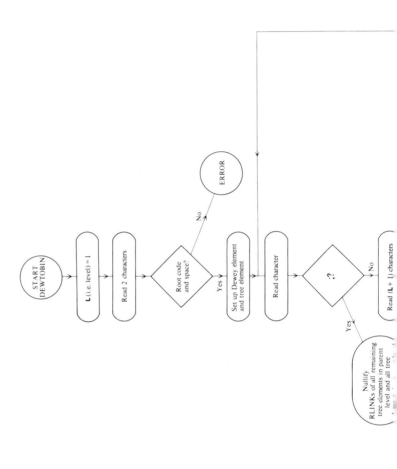

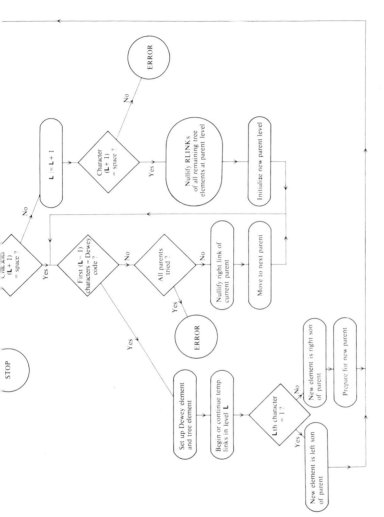

Fig. 4.14   Flowchart for Example 4.5

81

```
        COMMENT PLACE DEWEY CODE OF NEW ELEMENT IN
            STRING S;
        S := "␣";
        FOR J := 0 UNTIL L − 2 DO S(J|1) := B(I + J|1);
        WHILE S ¬= CODE(D0) DO
        BEGIN COMMENT LOOK FOR NEW PARENT;
            IF RLINK(T0) = NULL THEN ERROR(4)
            D0 := RLINK(T0);
            RLINK(T0) := NULL;
            T0 := ELT(D0)
        END;
        S(L − 1|1) := B(I + L − 1|1);

        COMMENT PLACE NEW DEWEY CODE AND DATUM IN
            LINE;
        D1 := DEWEY(S,NULL);
        IF D = NULL THEN D := D1    COMMENT START NEW
            LINE;
            ELSE RLINK(T1) := D1;
        FOR J := 1 UNTIL L − 1 DO WRITEON(B(I + J|1));
            COMMENT ECHO NEW DATA;
        I := I + L − 1;
        NEXTCHAR;
        ELT(D1) := T1 := SYMELT(NULL, B(I|1),NULL);

        COMMENT LAST DIGIT OF CODE DETERMINES LEFT/
            RIGHT LINK NEEDED;
        IF CODE(D1)(L − 1|1) = "1" THEN LLINK(T0) := T1
                            ELSE BEGIN D0 := RLINK(T0);
                                RLINK(T0) := T1;
                                IF D0 ¬= NULL THEN
                                    T0 := ELT(D0)
                            END;
        NEXTCHAR;
    END;

    COMMENT AT END OF DATA CLOSE CURRENT LEVEL AND
        PARENT LEVEL;
    CLOSE(T0,D0);
    D1 := D;
    T1 := ELT(D1);
    CLOSE(T1,D1);
    U := TRUE;
EXIT:
END DEWTOBIN;
```

82

Two-way links for tree structures

The storage structures which have been described work well when the root of a tree or subtree is known and the object is to investigate the branches of that root − for instance, when looking in a catalogue to find books about a particular aspect of a subject − but no provision has been made for the opposite operation of finding the root when a branch element is known. Questions of this kind are 'who is the man responsible for this sub-department?' or 'what is the operator to be applied to this operand?'

One solution is to start at the initial root of the tree and carry out a systematic traversal until the known branch element is reached; since the traversal algorithm must recognize branch points, it is not difficult to maintain a 'trailing pointer' which records the current subroot at every stage of the traversal. But this approach can, of course, be very lengthy and the alternative is to introduce some form of two-way linkage into the storage structure, just as was done for a linear list.

The simplest method is to include a FATHER link in the representation of every element, thus giving immediate access from each element to its root, but this means a considerable increase (which may be as much as one third) in the space required to represent each element.

A compromise can be achieved by providing one FATHER link for each *family* of children or branches. This technique is particularly convenient if the tree has been represented by its 'naturally corresponding' binary tree (Fig. 4.15) since, in this representation, the RLINK field of the youngest son would normally be NULL, indicating that there are no further brothers. Instead, this field can be used to contain a FATHER link, provided that a one-bit FLAG field can be made available in each element to distinguish between FATHER and BROTHER links. In other words, if the storage structure for the tree is increased by one bit per element (instead of one field per element) a FATHER link for each family can then be set up. The same principle can be applied if a tree is represented with each element in 'structured' form, as in Fig. 2.19.

Notice that a knowledge of all FATHER links would be sufficient to define any tree structure (by a 'bottom-up' process) but, besides the inherent disadvantages of using only one-way links, this would be an impractical description of a tree because of the need to include every leaf node in the definition. When SON links are used, only the root node need be stated.

Threaded binary trees

The thoughtful reader will have recognized that the proliferation of leaf elements in tree structures leads to a large number of NULL fields in the corresponding storage structures. The technique used in the previous section to set up a FATHER link for a family can be extended to utilize a high proportion of the fields which would otherwise be NULL; the result is to create 'thread links' which enable a tree to be traversed without the need for a stack.

Suppose that operations on the binary tree shown in Fig. 4.16 require it to be

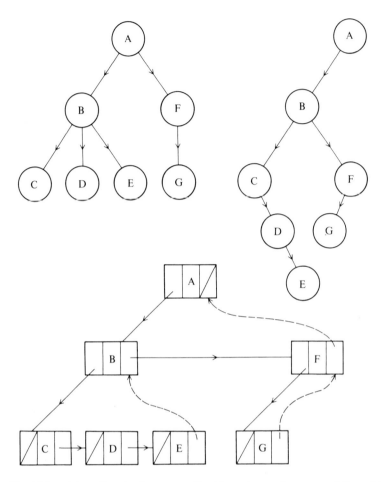

Fig. 4.15 A tree, its natural corresponding binary tree, and a representation which includes a FATHER link for each family in the tree

traversed symmetrically (which is BAEDFC). Wherever an element has no left (or right) son, the customary NULL link in the corresponding storage structure has been replaced by a link leading to the predecessor (or successor) of that element in a symmetric traversal (excepting the left and right fields respectively of the elements which occur first and last in symmetric order).

As before, it is necessary to associate a distinguishing one-bit FLAG field with each LINK field, but the threaded representation simplifies all search operations. Unfortunately Algol W does not allow one-bit fields, but suppose that the elements belong to the class

    RECORD THREADELT(REFERENCE(THREADELT) LLINK,RLINK;
        STRING(1) LFLAG,RFLAG,DATUM)

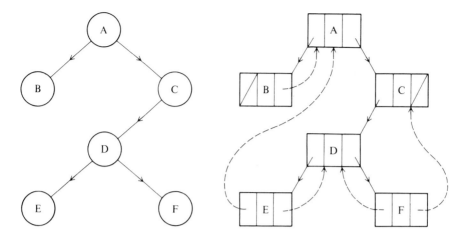

Fig. 4.16 A binary tree and its threaded representation

and let **FLAG** = "1" for a 'genuine' link and FLAG = "0" for a 'thread' link or NULL. Then, for example, the symmetric successor, S, of any element, T, is found by the procedure SUCCESSOR:

```
PROCEDURE SUCCESSOR(REFERENCE(THREADELT)S,T);
BEGIN S := RLINK(T); COMMENT SUCCESSOR FOUND IF THREAD
                                                LINK TAKEN;
     IF RFLAG(T) = "1" THEN WHILE LFLAG(S) = "1" DO
        S := LLINK(S);
END;
```

To traverse and print any binary threaded tree in symmetric order we first find the element which has no predecessor, and then all its successors. The algorithm is

```
WHILE LFLAG(T) = "1" DO T := LLINK(T);
WRITE (DATUM(T));
WHILE RLINK(T) ¬= NULL DO BEGIN SUCCESSOR(S,T);
                               T := S;
                               WRITE(DATUM(T));
                          END;
```

Compared to the traversal of an unthreaded binary tree, the space saved by dispensing with a stack can be very considerable and may require no more than two bits per element. Since stack operations are more complicated than the examination of a FLAG field, the algorithm will also be faster.

Thread links can also assist the task of finding the father of a given binary element: if the element, S, is a left son, and we descend from it as far as possible to the right, the father, T, is the next element in symmetric order, and hence

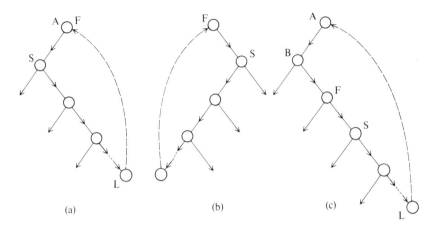

Fig. 4.17   The use of thread links to locate a FATHER element

accessed directly by the right-thread link (Fig. 4.17(a)). The corresponding case with left and right interchanged and the father as a predecessor in symmetric order is shown in Fig. 4.17(b). Unfortunately, given only S, the decision may be taken to descend to the right from S, although S is, if the full picture were known, itself a right son, leading typically to Fig. 4.17(c).

In general, assume that a series of *right* links has been followed from S, and that A is the element reached by the right thread link from L. Then either A ≡ F or, referring to Fig. 4.17(c),

1 F → S → · · · → L → A in symmetric order; i.e., F precedes A and must be in the left subtree of A;
2 there can be no node C between A and B, since C, not A, would then be the successor of L;
3 there can be no node D between F and B where a left link must be taken, for then D would follow L in symmetric order.

Hence an algorithm to locate the father, F, of a given element, S, of a binary tree T is

```
Z := S;
WHILE RFLAG(Z) = "1" DO Z = RLINK(Z);
F := RLINK(Z);    COMMENT FOLLOW THREAD LINK;
IF F = NULL THEN Z := T ELSE Z := LLINK(F);
IF Z ¬= S THEN BEGIN F := Z;
                     WHILE RLINK(F) ¬= S DO F := RLINK(F);
             END;
```

Notice that if S lies on the rightmost branches of the tree, the thread link which is reached is the final null value. In this case, the trace restarts from the root, T. In the special case when S = T initially, the result is F = NULL.

A similar algorithm can be devised using a leftwards descent from S; although these algorithms do not in general find F directly, they do locate the father of an element when the basic binary representation is enhanced only by the thread flags, which demand significantly less space than a FATHER link.

This discussion of threaded binary trees has concentrated entirely on a symmetric mode of traversal, but the principle is equally applicable to traversal in preorder or other orders. In general tree structures, the nodes do not have a regular format, and thread links cannot be added as readily, although the method which provided a link to the father of a family is of this type. The chief disadvantage in the use of binary threaded trees is the greater effort needed to add or delete items of the binary tree: beside resetting the genuine links, it may be necessary to trace predecessor or successor elements so that threaded links can be corrected.

Problems

4.1 Suppose that the sequential area defined by the array BLOCK (p. 55) is to be used (in a cyclic manner) to represent a deque. Are any of the algorithms for a stack or queue, as stated on pp. 55 and 56, also applicable to a deque? Say which, if any, these are and write any further algorithms which are necessary to provide the complete set of four basic addition and deletion operations for the deque.

4.2 A program is to read a set of integers in the range 0–49 and distribute them onto five stacks for units, tens, twenties, etc. A negative integer, $-i$, in the data indicates that the top element of stack i is to be printed and deleted ($1 \leqslant i \leqslant 5$). The integer 50 indicates the end of the set of integers. Any integer outside the range $(-5, 50)$ is to be reported as an error but otherwise ignored.

Use the array BLOCK (p. 55), with a suitable value of N, to simulate a sequential area available to the stacks, and provide two pointers for each stack to indicate the top of its allocated area and the position of its most recent element. State the initial values you assume for these pointers. If overflow occurs, allow one extra space to the stack which overflows, moving any adjacent stacks as necessary. Count the number of times that a stack has to be moved, and at the end of the data (or if an irrecoverable error occurs) print the total number of stack movements, the final contents of each stack, and the value of each pointer.

4.3 Repeat Problem 4.2 but, if a stack overflows, allow it (a) three extra spaces, (b) 10 per cent more space than its present size, and compare the number of stack movements involved.

4.4 A sequential area of space is shared between n stacks, and the space for *every* stack is reallocated whenever any one of them overflows. At each reallocation, 10 per cent of the total remaining free space is shared equally among the stacks, and the other 90 per cent is distributed in proportion to the amount by which a stack has increased in size since the previous reallocation. Write an algorithm for this method.

(This is Garwick's method of space allocation: see *BIT,* 4, 137–140 (1964), and Knuth (1973) pp. 244–6.)

4.5 Write an algorithm for joining a linear list L2 to the end of a linear list L1 so as to form a single list L.

4.6 Reverse the order of a linear list L without creating any new elements. Two temporary pointers may be used, and afterwards L should point to the new first element.

4.7 Write an algorithm to compare two linear lists L1, L2, checking that they have the same number of elements, and deleting from both lists any elements in corresponding positions of the lists whose DATUM fields are identical.

4.8 In a two-way list, show how to add an extra element containing the datum "V" immediately before an element of the list which contains datum "X". Remember that this element may occur at any point in the list.

4.9 The membership lists of two societies form two distinct sets of elements. Write a program to examine the lists and delete any people who are members of both societies. The program should print the names of those deleted, and the final membership of each society.

(Hint: represent each membership as a circular list.)

4.10 Describe briefly the use of circularly linked and doubly linked lists.

Select a representation for the terms of a polynomial in x, y and z. Give briefly the reasons for your choice and illustrate the representation for the polynomials

$$P \equiv x^3yz^2 - 2x^2y + 3yz + 4z^2$$
$$Q \equiv x^6 + x^2y + 3yz - z^4.$$

Outline an algorithm to find the difference of two such polynomials in the form

$$P := P - Q$$

(Queen Mary College, London, 1974)

4.11 Write a recursive procedure to output a binary tree in parentheses format.

4.12 Write an algorithm to output a binary tree structure in levelorder, with the value of each node accompanied by its appropriate Dewey code number.

4.13 Write a procedure which will print the contents of a binary tree in a manner which displays its structure. For example, the binary tree in Fig. 4.16 could be printed as

((B) A (((E) D (F)) C))

or as

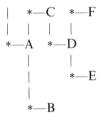

(Cambridge, 1973)

4.14 A binary tree is used to sort and store a set of objects, each of which has an associated integer reference number, or 'key'. At the start the tree is empty. As each item is added, it is placed at a tip of the tree so that, at any moment, the keys of the items in the left subtree of *any* node are all less than or equal to the key of the item at the node which, in turn, is less than the keys of all the nodes in its right subtree.

Find an algorithm which adds a new node to the tree, and another one which removes from the tree the node with the smallest key. By using the latter repeatedly, output the set of objects in increasing order of key magnitude.

(St Andrews, 1972)

4.15 Does every general binary tree correspond to some tree structure? When a correspondence exists, is it unique? Either give a counter-example or state an unambiguous rule for the transformation of a binary tree into a tree structure.

4.16 A tree structure has been represented as a general binary tree. Write an algorithm to traverse the binary tree and output the data in the levelorder of the *original* tree, with the value of each node accompanied by its Dewey code number in the tree structure.

4.17 A binary tree is stored in a standard format without any 'FATHER' links. By using a systematic traversal method, find and print the predecessor of an element whose DATUM value is given. Provision should be made for printing an error message if, for any reason, the predecessor cannot be found.

4.18 Explain what is meant by a binary tree structure which is 'threaded' in symmetric order. What are the advantages of this as compared with a conventional binary representation?

Write algorithms which, given an element P of the threaded binary tree, will find

(a) T1, the symmetric order successor of P
(b) T2, the symmetric order predecessor of P
(c) T3, the preorder successor of P.

Illustrate each answer with simple diagrams of the possible positions of P and T1, T2, and T3. Show that three diagrams are sufficient in each case.

(Bristol, 1974)

4.19 Given a binary tree which is threaded in symmetric order, write algorithms for the following operations:

(a) Insert an element V as the right subordinate of the existing element U in the tree; if U has an existing right subtree then this is to become the right subtree of V, otherwise V is to be a leaf element.
(b) Delete a leaf element U from the tree.

4.20 Write an algorithm to insert threads, for symmetric traversal, in an unthreaded binary tree.

(Glasgow, 1973)

4.21 Consider the following objection to the use of threaded binary trees to facilitate traversing algorithms:

'They are useless, because the extra space taken up by the thread pointers is more than would be used by a stack in implementing the simple recursive traversal algorithm.'

Give arguments against this view.

(Essex, 1974)

5. Provision of storage space for linked structures

When data are stored sequentially and are not subject to structural change, blocks of space are reserved by, for example, an ARRAY declaration in an Algol program or a DIMENSION statement in Fortran. Within a program, further space may be required and will be claimed by further declarations (or their equivalent), but since no structural changes take place, this further space can be allocated adjacent to previous areas. Even when data are subject to structural change, the advantages of direct rather than indirect (linked) access may lead to the use of an array to describe a sequential storage area, within which the space currently occupied will also be clearly delimited (Fig. 5.1). Thus, whenever sequential storage structures are used, the free space available for new data is always next to existing data in some sense (provided any free space remains).

In a linked storage structure, this simple situation cannot be maintained. Initially all the (linked) elements in use may be adjacent to each other in the store, but if there is a new value relevant to any part of the structure, it may be stored in any available location and correctly ordered merely by setting up appropriate links. Similarly, if elements become redundant the necessary links are changed to bridge the gap that has been created, but no attempt is made to 'close' the gap. Thus, the total area available for storage of the data structure rapidly becomes fragmented, with 'holes' of free space occurring within predominantly occupied areas and disjoint areas being used for the representation of connected structures.

In this situation, the only way in which free space can be recognized and supplied when needed is to apply the philosophy of the storage structures to the structure of free space, and maintain a *free list* which links together all areas of the total space which are available for use at any given stage of operations.

The reader may wonder why there has been no mention of a free list in the examples given hitherto. The answer is that the Algol W system (and most other

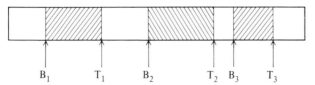

Fig. 5.1   Sequential storage structures within an array area

high-level programming systems which allow the use of linked data structures) maintains a free list on behalf of the user and provides free space when necessary; the statement which instructs it to do so is the 'record designator', e.g.,

JAMES := STUDENT;

or

ICI := COMPANY ("ICI", "TEESIDE");

Knowing the format of each record class from its initial declaration (which does *not* create an instance of the class), the system can now set aside an appropriate area of store, within which the fields may or may not be defined, and plant the address of this area in the stated reference variable. Similarly, when a user deletes an element from a list, it is left to the system to determine whether the element is an integral part of any other structure and, if not, to make this space available (in a manner to be discussed) for alternative use.

An automatic store maintenance system of this kind is very convenient for the user, but it is reasonable to ask whether it is less efficient than providing explicit access to a list of free space. It is probably true that a skilful and knowledgeable programmer could find ways to economize his store requirements, and possibly thereby reduce the run time of the program as compared with the automated system. But not all users have this detailed knowledge or the time to apply it, and a saving in human resources can readily outweigh marginal technical gains. The argument is similar to the case for a high-level programming language in preference to assembly code programming, and as systems and data structures become more complex, it is progressively less likely that an individual user can fully grasp the relationships of the overall picture. An analogy may perhaps be drawn with the automatic landing systems which are used in modern aircraft, because they can react more quickly than a human pilot to the rapidly changing situation of the aircraft in relation to the ground and other aircraft.

Form of the free list
When it is necessary to claim space for a new element, a block of free space must be accessed and the space it contains compared with the amount required. If all the elements of a storage structure are of a uniform size, and the total space initially is a multiple of this size, then this property remains true for all free blocks. In this case, having located a free block, it is sufficient to decrement its size without further examination, since space is claimed element by element, and if a free block exists it must contain sufficient space for at least one new element of the standard size. When the block has been fully used it is deleted from the free list. More easily, the free list can be a simple linear list of areas, each sufficient to hold one standard element, thus obviating the need for an explicit size field in each area.

If, however, the structure contains elements of varying sizes, an area of free space which has been located may be too small to accommodate the type of element to be created; indeed, it may prove impossible to find any contiguous area large enough, even though the free space as a whole significantly exceeds the size of the required element. There is no simple solution to the problem of store fragmentation caused by varying-sized elements. When only a limited number of sizes can occur, a partial solution is to set up a separate free list for each size, possibly also restricting each category to its own partition of the total store; this makes the provision of free space for a new element very much easier, but does not resolve the problem of one free list becoming empty while free space still exists elsewhere. The only complete answer is to reorganize the store periodically, 'compacting' all space currently in use and leaving the remainder as a contiguous free area. There will be many cross-references among the elements, all of which have to be readjusted; these corrections will have to be calculated individually, since the storage area in use is being compressed and not simply relocated *en bloc*, as when a program is loaded into store. Store compaction can become essential, but it is not a step to be undertaken lightly. Fortunately 'housekeeping operations' such as this are normally the responsibility of the operating system rather than the user.

Maintenance of free lists

Given that at least one free list exists, how can it (or they) be maintained? In other words, how are they replenished as the release of elements makes space available? There are two possibilities. (1) Detect all deletion operations as they occur, check that the deleted element is not a member of any other structures and, if not, attach it to a free list. (2) Ignore all deleted elements until all known free space has been claimed, trace through all structures as they then exist, marking their constituent elements, then link all unmarked elements to recreate a free list.

Method (1) is perhaps the more obvious approach, and was used in some early structure-processing systems: a special field associated with each element or group of elements is incremented by one for every reference made to that element or group, and decremented by one when a link is broken; when and only when a 'reference count' reaches zero, that element or group can be returned to the end of the free list. For the structure shown in Fig. 5.2, if the link GH is broken, the element H can be returned, and if the link CD is broken, the element D can be returned. In the latter case, the link DG is redundant because the element D can no longer be accessed, but it is easier not to reduce the reference count of G to one until the space occupied by D is re-used — this postpones the need to trace any substructures of a deleted element.

There are a number of disadvantages in the counter method: space is required for the counter fields, time is spent adjusting a counter field whenever a link is changed, and circular or recursive structures cannot be deleted without special treatment, because they always generate their own reference count.

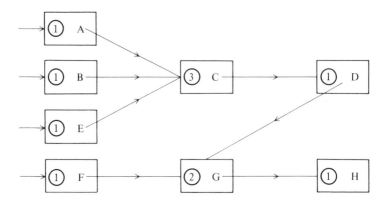

Fig. 5.2 Linked structure including 'reference count' fields

Method (2), which takes no action until all free space has been used and then sweeps up all space which cannot be traced through some structure, has inevitably acquired the name of *garbage collection*. For this method, the counter field is replaced by a one-bit marker field for each element (all such bits can, if desirable, be collected in a marker map separated from the element space), and no overheads whatever are incurred unless or until an overflow situation occurs. A further incidental advantage is that the trace routine which is an integral part of the garbage collector can also be invoked as a useful debugging aid. The chief drawbacks of the method are the fact that it must, by hypothesis, operate in a minimal storage area, tending to make it slow in operation, and the difficulty of designing the trace algorithm so that it can accept elements of any size and format defined by the user.

Methods of garbage collection
Any linked storage structure will be accessed via a number of reference variables (sometimes called 'base registers') leading to substructures which may or may not be disjoint. Each of these substructures must be traced by a garbage collector, starting at the base register and continuing until the structure has been fully traced (i.e., NULL links found) or a previously marked structure is entered. If a NULL link is regarded as leading to a permanently marked 'element', the process can be described in outline by the flowchart in Fig. 5.3.

The flowchart implies that the garbage collector can recognize those fields of an element which represent link variables, and this information will be gained from the record-class declaration in Algol W or a corresponding source. The crucial problem is how to 'remember' branch points while tracing each of their branches. In other circumstances, such as the traversal of a tree structure, the use of a stack would be a simple solution, but it must be remembered that a garbage collector *cannot* be allowed unlimited work space. In a 'pathological' case, a

94

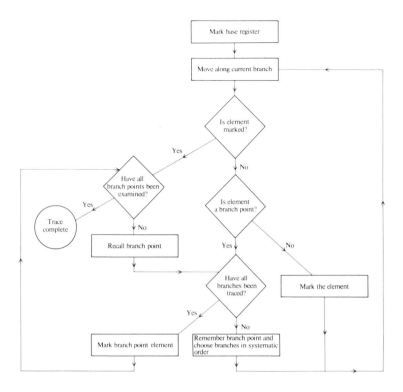

Fig. 5.3   Outline of trace routine for garbage collection

stack might acquire as many entries as the structure being traced: consider the structure S in Fig. 5.4, and suppose that in each element the fields are selected from right to left; each element is recognized as a branch point and hence 'remembered', since the NULL value of each left link is not detected until all the right links have been traced.

This example points a warning, but when extended to the full size of the available store, such a structure could be ignored on probabilistic grounds, and it is possible for a garbage collector to use a stack with an upper bound placed on the size of the stack; if the stack becomes full before tracing is complete, processing is abandoned. Knuth has described a variation of this method, which falls back on a sequential scan of the store if the stack overflows, thus avoiding a premature termination of processing (see Problem 5.3).

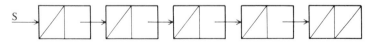

Fig. 5.4

Garbage collection without a stack

However there is a much more convenient method, first described by H. Schorr and W. M. Waite (1967), which needs no auxiliary stack and is able to trace circular or recursive structures.

MARK (1 bit)	DATUM		MARK (1 bit)	BRANCH (1 bit)	LLINK	RLINK

Format of leaf element.   Fig. 5.5   Format of simple node element.

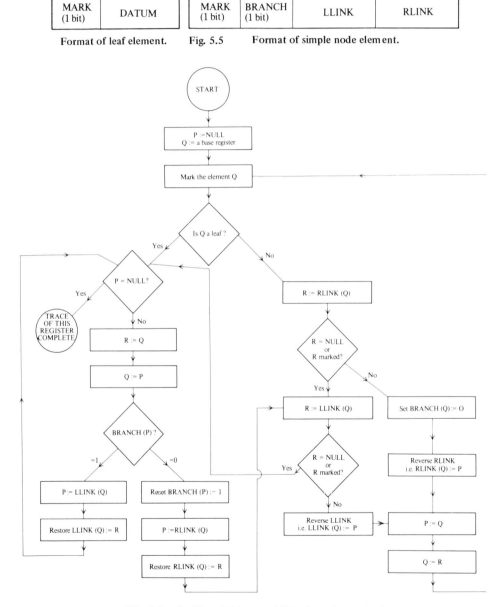

Fig. 5.6   Outline of Schorr and Waite's tracing method

96

For each base register of a structure, the principle is to *reverse* the links as a branch is traced and marked; when a leaf or a previously marked element is reached, the trace steps back to the nearest branch point, resetting the modified links to their proper states. Each branch in turn is traced in this way and 'branch bits' indicate which branch is being traced and consequently which link field of the branch point is currently reversed.

As a simple example, suppose that every element is either a binary branch node or a leaf. As shown in Fig. 5.5, every element is given a MARK bit and each branch node has a BRANCH field which, in this case, also consists of a single bit. Initially MARK = 0 and BRANCH = 1. The algorithm sets MARK = 1 when an element is traced, and also temporarily modifies BRANCH while tracing a RLINK so that the value of BRANCH can be used to determine whether a right or left link is to be reset during the restoration stage. The flow chart is shown in Fig. 5.6, and initially Q = a base register, P = NULL.

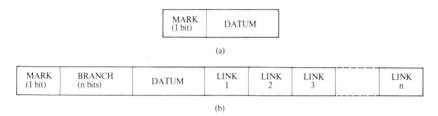

Fig. 5.7   (a) Format of leaf element. (b) Format of general node element

In a general case, we may assume that elements have one of the formats shown in Fig. 5.7, where MARK is again a one-bit field which is initially zero and the BRANCH field of a node has as many binary ones as the node has link fields. The algorithm could be described concisely by a recursive procedure, but this would, in effect, re-introduce the stack which this method is designed to avoid. The procedure TRACE is therefore written instead as an iterative routine. It uses a subsidiary procedure ZERO(Q) which has an integer value equal to the number of zero bits in the BRANCH field of Q, and Algol W notation has been slightly extended so that LINK(Q,J) refers to the Jth link field of the node Q and BITVALUE(Q,J) refers to the Jth bit of the BRANCH field.

Initially TRACE is called with Q = a base register and P = NULL.

```
PROCEDURE TRACE(REFERENCE(LEAF,NODE)Q,P);
BEGIN REFERENCE(LEAF,NODE)R;
        INTEGER J;
FLAG:MARK(Q) := 1;    COMMENT MARK ELEMENT AS TRACED;
TEST: IF Q IS NODE THEN
        BEGIN NEXT:IF BRANCH(Q) = 0 THEN GOTO RESET;
             COMMENT ALL BRANCHES TRACED?;
          J := ZERO(Q) + 1;  COMMENT PREPARE TO TRACE
                              BRANCH J;
```

```
          BITVALUE(Q,J) := 0;    COMMENT SET BIT TO ZERO
              THEN TRACE CORRESPONDING LINK;
          R := LINK(Q,J);
          IF (R = NULL) OR (MARK(R) = 1) THEN GOTO NEXT;
          LINK(Q,J) := P;   COMMENT REVERSE LINK;
          P := Q;           COMMENT MOVE ALONG BRANCH;
          Q := R;
          GOTO FLAG;
    RESET: J := 1;          COMMENT RESET ALL BRANCH BITS
                                TO ONE;
          WHILE ZERO(Q) ¬= 0 DO
          BEGIN BITVALUE(Q,J) := 1;
              J := J + 1
          END
    END;
    IF P ¬= NULL THEN COMMENT WHEN PREDECESSOR IS NULL
        TRACE IS COMPLETE;
    BEGIN J := ZERO(P);   COMMENT J FIXES LINK TO BE RESET;
          R := Q;         COMMENT R,Q,P MOVE BACK ONE
                                STEP;
          Q := P;
          P := LINK(Q,J);
          LINK(Q,J) := R;   COMMENT RESET LINK;
          GOTO TEST
    END
END TRACE;
```

The garbage collector for the Algol W system uses Schorr and Waite's method essentially as described above, though it assigns a separate 'page' or 'pages' of store to each class of records. When the collector is called and has traced all records in use, all free records on a page are linked together. If any page contains no records in use, it is attached to a list of free pages, and any free pages adjacent to the sequential free area (used for arrays and simple variables) are amalgamated with that area. This segregation of areas reduces store fragmentation, provides resources for both sequential and linked structures, yet enables space to be found quickly for records of any type by the following steps:

1 examine the free list on the current page of the record class;
2 if the page is full, examine the list of free pages and allocate a new page if possible;
3 otherwise claim space for a new page from the sequential area adjacent to existing pages.

Garbage collection and store reallocation
It should be recognized that the tracing and collection of garbage does nothing to remove the fragmentation of free space which develops in the storage area as a

structure changes dynamically. This is of little consequence if all new records require space of a uniform size (as happens on any one page of the Algol W system), but in other cases it may be necessary to reorganize the store after collecting garbage. The space still required can then, as suggested on p. 93, be compacted together so as to release a contiguous free area. A more general garbage collector of this type thus has four phases:

> trace all current structures;
> link all remaining space and calculate its total size;
> calculate a new position for every current record and adjust all pointers accordingly;
> move all current records to their new positions.

The details of such methods are beyond the scope of this book, but an example has been described by Wegbreit (1972).

Needless to say, store reorganization adds considerably to the time already required for tracing. Indeed, a word of warning applicable to all forms of garbage collection is that the operation may not be worthwhile when the remaining free space becomes very limited. This condition is often the result of an undetected error but, whatever the cause, there is very little room for manoeuvre. A dynamic structure, having emptied a free list once in these circumstances, is likely to do so again quite quickly, and to avoid repeated calls of the garbage collector (which may ultimately prove fruitless) it is often simpler to abandon processing when the collection of garbage at any stage yields less than a fixed minimum quantity of space.

Dynamic block allocation

Another problem involving dynamic structures is the allocation of blocks of space by an operating system in a multi-programming environment. In such a system, programs or partial programs reside on auxiliary storage until required for processing, at which point a sufficiently large free area of main store must be found and made available. One method is to arrange that all programs can be regarded as occupying one or more 'pages' of a uniform size in the auxiliary store, so that main-store allocation is reduced to keeping a table of those 'page frames' in the main store which are currently free.

When a paging system is not used, the free areas of the main store must be explicitly linked, because of their varied sizes and the unpredictable manner in which they occur as active processes enter and leave the main store. The problem is to maintain this list of free space.

When compared with the elements of a dynamic data structure, the process-blocks entering the store have a quite arbitrary size. A second major difference is that a data structure is normally allowed a reasonable quantity of free space for its development, whereas the store available for process-blocks is regarded as a valuable resource to be utilized as fully as possible. This means that garbage collector methods, which postpone the reclamation of space, are quite inappropriate. Nor are reference counters useful, since the number of references to a process is generally of less interest than the question of whether *any* reference has been made in the recent past. Instead, a block of space becomes available for re-use when a process terminates, or is stalled for any reason, or when no references are made to this block within a predetermined time.

The store-maintenance routine must accept a newly released block, determine whether there are adjacent blocks already free with which it can be amalgamated, and attach the amalgamated block at a suitable point in the list of free blocks. (The choice of a suitable point depends in part on the way the list is maintained and used.) The routine must also find and deliver a block of sufficient size, whenever space is required for a new process in the main store. Because of the importance of utilizing the main store efficiently, both the acceptance and the release of space should be carried out as quickly as possible, and the free list must be organized with this in mind. It could be arranged with blocks in the order

1 of their size, or
2 of their position in the main store, or
3 in which they were released.

As so often happens, none of these is entirely satisfactory: (1) simplifies the delivery of a suitable block on demand, but the list must be fully searched when attempting to consolidate a newly released block with existing free blocks; (2), on the other hand, simplifies the acceptance of a block which has been released, but makes it difficult to decide which block to supply on demand; (3) is a method which has been used in conjunction with dynamic structures whose elements are predictable in size, but in the present context it combines the disadvantages of (1) and (2).

The choice between (1) and (2) can be described as a choice between 'best fit' and 'first fit' methods: since a store request does not, in general, exactly match any available block, should one find the nearest (larger) size or accept *any* block which is large enough? The first choice avoids the destruction of some potentially useful large free area (but may lead to a proliferation of valueless 'offcuts'); the second makes no attempt to match the sizes requested and available, but allows the free list to be organized in form (2) which is the more convenient when blocks are released.

If it were true that use of the 'best-fit' method would maintain a more flexible supply of free space than the 'first-fit' method, and thereby allow processing to continue more freely, the choice would be difficult, but this is not necessarily the case, and on other grounds the latter method is the more efficient in operation. Details of algorithms based on this method are given by Knuth (1973).

The buddy system

A quite different approach to block allocation, which offers a possible compromise between the first-fit and best-fit methods, is the so-called *buddy*

Initial state

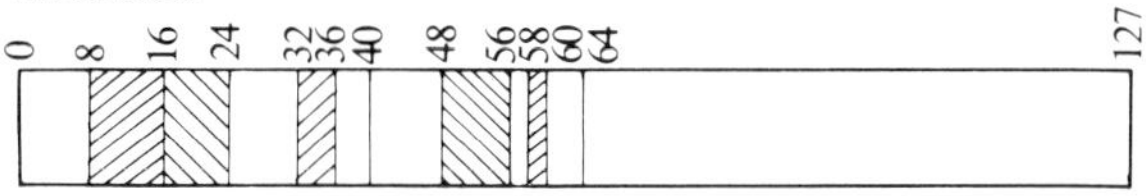

Block size	Free addresses initially	After request for 14 locations	After release of locations 32–35
128	NIL	NIL	NIL
64	64	NIL	NIL
32	NIL	96	96
16	NIL	80	32,80
8	0, 24, 40	0, 24, 40	0, 24
4	36, 60	36, 60	60
2	56	56	56

Final state

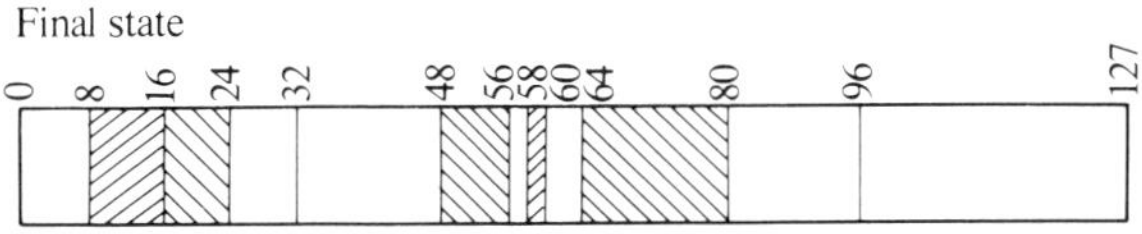

Fig. 5.8   An example of the operation of the buddy system

system. In this, space is always allocated in blocks whose size is a power of 2, and separate free lists are maintained for each of these sizes. Store requests are rounded up to the next larger power of 2 and, if no block of this size is free, the next larger block is halved, and one half halved again until a block of the required size is obtained. Initially, the store is regarded as a single free block, and since all smaller blocks arise from binary fission, each one has a natural pair or 'buddy'. If or when a block and its buddy are both unused, they are fused to recreate a single larger block (which may lead to further fusion). To maintain the symmetry, blocks which are not buddies may not be fused, even though they may be adjacent, both free, and of equal size; such blocks remain on their respective free lists. By this means, the system attempts to maintain a reserve of large free blocks and encourage the use of blocks which as nearly as possible match the store requested.

To illustrate the method, Fig. 5.8 shows a typical state of a small store of 128 locations, and the effect on the free lists of a request for 14 locations (rounded up to 16) followed by the release of 4 locations currently in use.

The buddy system requires the explicit release of available space, but places more emphasis on free lists than the block methods discussed in the previous section. Thus, it is particularly appropriate in conjunction with a low-level programming system or for applications in which data occur in blocks whose size varies dynamically — by contrast to the data structures considered in chapter 4, where the elements were generally fixed in size but members of dynamically variable structures.

101

Problems

5.1 Suppose that every element has four fields, COUNT, DATUM, LLINK, and RLINK, where the value of COUNT is the number of references (pointers) to the element. When an element becomes redundant, is it better to attach it to the front or to the rear of the free list? Give reasons for your choice and write the appropriate routines (a) to return an element T to the free list, (b) to claim an element from the free list and assign it to the pointer T.

Using these routines, write algorithms for the following operations:

   (i)   insert a new element T immediately to the right of an element P of an existing list;

   (ii) remove from a list the element T which is immediately to the right of an element P of the list, returning T to the free list if appropriate;

  (iii) make two existing lists L and R the sublists of a new element T.

(You may assume that all lists use one-way links, and that no circular lists occur.)

5.2 Suppose that every element in a storage structure is either a branch point or a leaf (i.e., it has one of the formats in Fig. 5.5, excluding the BRANCH bit). Mark all elements to which the initial reference variables (the base registers) point directly, and devise an algorithm that will trace all other accessible elements by making repeated sequential scans through the available storage space; each scan is to look for marked elements which are branch points, and mark their subelements (if these are not already marked).

Would it ever be possible to complete the trace in one scan? Could it ever require n scans, where n is the number of elements in the data? Say what the storage structure would be for either case to be possible.

5.3 Assume that elements have the same format as in Problem 5.2, and use the base registers to mark an initial set of elements as before. Write an algorithm that will trace all other accessible elements, given that up to T elements may be placed on a temporary stack during the trace operation in order to avoid or reduce the need for repeated sequential scans of the store.

(cf. Knuth (1973), Algorithm C, p. 415.)

5.4 Outline Schorr and Waite's method for garbage collection. Draw a state diagram (a digraph) to illustrate the operation of a double-switched light circuit, as used between two floors of a house, and verify that the algorithm is capable of tracing all the elements in this structure. (Assume that the initial state is when both switches are 'up' and the light is off.)

5.5 (a) Can Schorr and Waite's method be used to trace structures in which the number of link fields in an element (including NULL values) is not uniform? State any additional assumption or requirement you would wish to make in this case and, if necessary, indicate how the procedure TRACE should be modified.

   (b) How could the BRANCH field be used to distinguish between leaf and node elements if the predicate IS was unavailable (i.e., the programming language was unable to determine the class of record to which a reference refers).

5.6 Why is it necessary to maintain a list of available space when using a linked storage allocation scheme?

   Describe in detail how you would implement an available space list, pointed to by the link variable AVAIL, when it is not known in advance how much space will be needed for all the lists, and when a sequential table of variable size must also coexist with the linked structures. In the description you are expected to consider the operations

$$X := AVAIL \qquad and \qquad AVAIL := X,$$

which are, respectively, macros for setting a link variable X to the address of a new element, and for returning an element pointed to by X to the available space list.

(Brighton Polytechnic, 1974)

5.7 Describe what is meant by *dynamic storage allocation* and explain why the techniques of garbage collection are inappropriate in this context.

   Suppose that the available free store, in positional order, consists of blocks of 50, 200, 100, and 150 locations respectively. Verify that it is possible to receive a sequence of four (or more) requests for space, all of which can be met if a 'first-fit' allocation algorithm is used, but the last of which fails if a 'best-fit' method is used.

5.8 In a dynamic storage allocation scheme all blocks contain a SIZE field, and all free blocks contain LLINK and RLINK fields to form a two-way list of all free blocks, which is maintained in the order of their position in the store. Write algorithms (a) to obtain a block of N free locations using the first-fit method, and (b) to release a block of N locations commencing at location L. In the latter case ensure that any adjacent free blocks are merged with the new area.

   You may assume in this question

   (a) that a reference variable is not restricted to a fixed size of block,
   (b) that it is possible to add an integer variable to a reference variable, thus obtaining a new reference value.

5.9 Consider the following objection to the buddy-system algorithm for returning a block to free storage:

'It won't work, because when the address of the buddy of the block is calculated, that might give a location in the *middle* of a *larger* block, which might itself be in use.'

Show that this objection is groundless.

(Essex, 1974)

5.10 Explain the principles of the 'buddy' system of store allocation. Why is this type of system likely to be more useful than a garbage collector when store requests are for areas of varying sizes?

Write algorithms that use the buddy system (a) to meet a request for n words of store, assuming that the total storage is 2^m words and that $0 < n < 2^m$, and (b) to release a block of 2^k words starting at location L, assuming that $k < m$. State clearly any assumptions you make about the format of blocks or the initial values of pointers.

(Bristol, 1974)

6. Tables and files

The characteristics of tabular information

A table was defined in chapter 1 as a set of records having a common format, such as a tide table or a table of rail or air services. The word 'record' is not used here in the specialized sense of Algol W, but means merely an ordered set of items which need not be homogeneous in type, irrespective of the manner of storage. Subsequent chapters have emphasized that the choice of a representation for any structure must be strongly influenced by the nature of the operations to be carried out on it, and in the case of a table, the most common of these are referencing an entry or adding a new entry as a table is being created. It is often necessary to amend a field of an entry (which implies a reference to the table), but the deletion of a complete entry is a less frequent operation. In the following discussion it may be helpful to bear in mind some examples of situations in which information in a tabular form occurs:

1 The construction of a symbol table during the assembly or compilation of a computer program; as each user-defined symbol or name is encountered, the table is searched to see whether an entry for this symbol already exists as a result of a previous reference to it, and if not, an entry is created which associates the symbol with a location in store.
2 A table of hotel accommodation within some area, containing details such as name of hotel, nearest town, postal address and telephone number, number of bedrooms and bathrooms, cost of accommodation, whether a lift is available, etc.
3 A 'switching table' which associates a set of possible values in a computer program with a set of mutually exclusive labels, statements, or procedures.
4 A tide table, containing the times and heights of high tide for each day.
5 A set of essential information about the employees of a company, such as name, department, insurance number, tax code, salary grade, total pay and tax in the current year. In principle, this is very similar to (2), but for a large company the volume of information is much greater, necessitating the use of non-random-access store, and the set is called a *file*. Access to the file, however, uses an auxiliary table in the main store.

Setting aside the possibility of deletions for a moment, it is possible to distinguish between tables which are fixed in the sense that all their entries are complete, and those which are still being created and therefore dynamic; in the former case an ordering is possible, based on some field which is unlikely to change (a person's name, perhaps, or the registration number of a car), but in the latter case an ordering (though possible) is unlikely to be worthwhile. In either situation, the fact that an occasional entry has become obsolete can be indicated by a special one-bit field, to avoid the necessity for immediate reorganization of the tabular representation. A periodic check on the number of such obsolete entries indicates when the representation should be reconstructed.

As for any data structure, it is essential to associate an access algorithm with the representation of a table. Access could be by position within the representation — 'find the fourth record in the table' — but this takes no account of the contents of the record, and the fact that each record can be a set of values (unlike an element in an array) means that the records can usually be ordered in a number of different ways. Instead, a reference is normally based on some aspect of an entry in the table — 'find the make of car whose registration number is ABC123Z' — and the basis of the enquiry (the registration number in this example) is known as the 'key' of the entry or record. Sometimes the key can be used as the argument of a function which calculates the address of the corresponding record; alternatively, associative access can be used — the key whose record is required is compared with the key of each record in turn until a match is found (or failure reported).

A record in a table may be identified by a number of its fields, according to the type of enquiry being made; for example, we may ask for a record 'with the name Arthur Robinson', or 'with the insurance number ABC12Z3', or 'with the occupation of programmer'. Not all of these are necessarily able or intended to identify a *unique* record and, in a sequential storage structure, only one of the fields can be chosen as the key on which the table is ordered. Needless to say, an associative access can be more efficiently carried out when the field being searched has also been used as the key field on which the table is ordered, but it is an unfortunate fact that the same table must often be searched for more than one property. When the property sought is not the basis of the ordering, this leads to the problem of 'inverted files', which are discussed later in this chapter.

Storage structures for tables

When storing a table, it is not necessary to allow for the same degree of flexibility and volatility as was needed for many of the structures discussed in chapter 4. When a table is being created, it is often possible to place an upper bound on its size, and new entries are most commonly placed either in specific positions determined by their key, or added sequentially to existing records then sorted when the table is complete. Many operations access a value within a table (as in an array), but operations which change its structure, including the deletion of an entry, are comparatively rare. A further consideration is that the set of records in a table all have the same format, even though the individual content may be non-homogeneous in type (compare this with the arbitrary structure of a tree), and therefore the records can be of constant length, provided that an arbitrary upper limit is placed on such fields as name or address (as is common practice).

For these reasons, a table is normally stored as a sequential structure. This can be easily achieved when using a low-level programming language, where the reservation of a block of storage does not require or allow the specification of its future contents: these will be interpreted as numbers, characters, logical variables, etc., according to the operations carried out on them by the programmer; for example, a block of 100 machine words for 'TABLE' could be reserved by the typical assembly language statement

TABLE BSS 100

A high-level language imposes more restrictions on the programmer in the interests of brevity and accuracy, but at the cost of flexibility. The ability to set up an array of homogeneous data types is almost universal in high-level languages, but acceptance of a non-homogeneous sequential set to represent a table is very rare. It is possible in Algol 68 (see chapter 7), and in a number of other languages a structure of this type can be created in a more or less roundabout way; in Algol W, the entries in the table can be represented by RECORDS (of a class ENTRY, say) which are accessed via a REFERENCE ARRAY and created by a statement of the form

FOR I := 1 UNTIL N DO TABLE(I) := ENTRY

where TABLE is the name of the array. This creates a sequential area of non-homogeneous types, but at the cost of an additional level of access — first to the array, and thence to the records.

Access methods

Address calculation

It was shown in chapter 2 that the element A(i) of a one-dimensional array A can be accessed by the formula $A_0 + c * i$, where A_0 is the location of the first element A(0) and c is the space occupied by each element. This method is known as *address calculation*, and its direct access to any element gives sequential array storage its advantage in speed by comparison with linked structures. The same method gives the simplest and fastest access to tabular structures, but it is practicable only if the keys of the table are consecutive, or regularly spaced, or — at the least — occur densely within a range of values. In other situations, too high a proportion of the sequential area would correspond to non-relevant keys and remain unused.

A monthly tide table is an example in which address calculation is possible: each entry corresponds to a key (day-of-month) in the range 1–31, and only one of these keys (except in February) may not correspond to an entry in the table. Another example is the use of a switching table to implement statements such as 'COMPUTED GOTO' in Fortran or 'CASE' in Algol W: the current value of an integer variable is used to determine an entry in the table, and this contains the address of the statement to be executed next. Given the statement

GOTO (S1, S2, S3, . . ., SN), I

or

CASE (I) OF BEGIN S1; S2; S3; . . .; SN END

control goes to S3 if I = 3. (The value of I must lie in the range 1—N). Similarly, a table of costs when a discount is allowed for purchases in bulk may have entries for 5, 10, 15, 20, . . ., units; clearly the cost per unit of t units can be found in location $t_0 + t/5 - 1$, where t_0 is the first location of the table.

Address calculation can also be used when the keys are non-numeric, provided that a correspondence exists between the set of keys and a set of regularly spaced numbers: for example, the letters of the alphabet might correspond to the values 1—26. Notice that address calculation obviates the need to store the key of each record, as this is implicit in the position of the record in the sequential area. This is the only storage method in which the keys of a table can be omitted.

When the keys of a table are spaced in a manner which is only approximately regular, *address estimation* may be used to access a table which has been previously created and ordered. This is a variation of the previous method in which the probable location corresponding to a key is estimated and the key which is actually stored at this position is compared with the key required. The estimate may prove to be correct but, if not, adjacent keys are examined before or after this position in the table according to the result of the unsuccessful comparison. The objective of this method is to utilize the degree of regularity in the table to curtail the step-by-step searching which is a feature of other forms of access to an ordered table, as described below.

Sequential and binary searching

If the location which corresponds to a key cannot be calculated directly, the simplest (though usually not the fastest) associative method is to examine the key of each record in turn until one is found which matches the key required. Each step of this *sequential search* can be carried out very quickly, but since no account is taken of ordering, the average length of search is half the number of entries in the table.

If a table is ordered, the average length of search can be drastically reduced, at the cost of more complex and time-consuming operations at each step, by a *binary search*. The key to be found is compared with the key of a record at the middle of the table; if the comparison is unsuccessful, the process is then repeated with the 'upper' or 'lower' half of the table according to the result of the comparison. If the table contains n records, the required key can be found or its absence reported after at most $1 + \log_2 n$ such steps.

A binary search is the most efficient access method for large ordered tables when direct access is not possible, but the simple sequential search is faster for small tables (and does not require them to be ordered). The break-even point depends on the additional time needed at each step of a binary search to select and delimit one half of the table, and this varies with the computer available and the programming language used. If each step of a binary search is five times longer than each step of a sequential search, the break-even size is 22 entries; if the factor is only three, the critical size is reduced to 10 entries.

Random access using hash codes

Apart from a sequential search, all the access methods which have been described require a table to be ordered and are therefore unsuitable for a table which is being created and whose keys are not predictable in advance – for example the symbol table generated during a compilation process. It is possible to store the records sequentially in the order in which entries occur and sort them when they are complete, but this is inefficient if it is also necessary to refer to the table while it is incomplete (as in the case of a compiler's symbol table). What is required is a deterministic method of assigning a location to a record once its key is known, while recognizing that only a small proportion of the possible keys in a range are likely to occur in practice. (For example, if a user-defined symbol can consist of one to six upper case letters there are $26 + 26^2 + \cdots + 26^6 = 321\ 272\ 406$ different symbols possible.) In other words, we wish to map a sparse set of keys covering a very large domain on to a much smaller range where their images will occur more densely but, hopefully, without repetition.

The method used to solve this apparently intractable problem is known as *hash coding*, in which a transformation function is applied to the key of a record and the result determines the storage location to be used. The algorithms chosen accept that some repetition of results is almost inevitable and, rather than attempting to eliminate this entirely, such cases are specially treated. For simplicity, the method is described in terms of keys that are numeric, since alphabetic and other types of keys can be converted to numeric form by suitable coding.

A very simple hash function is to select only a subset of the digits of a key, for example the two least significant digits or the two middle digits from a set of six, leading to 'hash codes' in the range 0–99. However, if the six digits represent a date of birth (day, month, year) in the first half of this century, the resulting range is very limited: 0–49 or 1–12 respectively. This shows that any hash function must take some account of the known or probable distribution of the keys if it is to produce a random set of codes which span the range. In this example, the three dates concerned could instead be added to obtain a code in the range 2–92, (thus the key 10–12–24 would give the hash code 46). Hash functions in which certain digits are selected, or the digits are combined in some way, are said to 'cut' or 'fold' the key.

As an alternative problem, suppose that a table of European vehicle statistics

France	F	060000
Belgium	B	020000
Holland	NL	141200
Germany	D	040000
Great Britain	GB	070200
Ireland	IRL	091812
Italy	I	090000
Denmark	DK	041100

Fig. 6.1   Some international registration letters and their numeric equivalents

is to be collected, country by country, using the international registration letters
of each country as the keys. By converting each letter into a two-digit code
corresponding to its alphabetic position, we again obtain six-digit keys as shown
in Fig. 6.1, but in this table neither cutting nor folding provides a very suitable
hash code. The first digit pair could be cut to yield a hash code in the range
1–26, but a number of repetitions would arise from countries such as Germany
and Denmark, while folding the key in the manner used previously would
produce hash codes from 1 to 78, a range much larger than the number of
entries to be made in the table and therefore wasteful of space. Instead, the code
values can be restricted to any desired range by using 'residue arithmetic': for a
range of 19, assign locations in the storage structure according to the residues
when each key is divided by 19 (Fig. 6.2). A prime divisor is normally chosen to
avoid the obvious repetitions or 'collisions' which will occur if a number of keys
contain some common factor – any even divisor, and especially a multiple of 10,
would be ineffective if applied to the keys in Fig. 6.1. Even if the divisor (and
hence the size of the table) is prime, it is quite possible for a collision to
occur – Finland (SF), key 190600, gives the same hash code, 11, as Holland
when modulo 19 is used. But in most cases the ratio of the number of possible
keys to the number of probable keys is far too great to allow a unique storage
location or area to be assigned to each key, and hence collisions between hash
codes derived from the keys must be accommodated as much as avoided. It is
essential to devise a simple and efficient method for dealing with this problem if

Key	Hash code
060000	17
020000	12
141200	11
040000	5
070200	14
091812	4
090000	16
041100	3

Fig. 6.2   Hash codes generated by residues modulo 19

hash functions are to be of practical value in creating and accessing a tabular storage structure.

Progressive overflow in hash-coded tables

When a collision occurs, an 'overflow' location or area must be defined. The simplest solution is to attempt to place the tabular entry corresponding to the most recent (colliding) key in the position following its 'home' position; if this is also occupied, move on a further step until an empty location is found. (The position of an entry may involve a single location or several.)

In the previous example suppose that entries for Norway(N), Finland(SF), Spain(E), and Czechoslovakia(CZ) are added to those already present, as shown by the capitals in Fig. 6.3. The Norwegian entry can be placed without difficulty at the first attempt, but the home base for Finland is 11, which is already occupied by the entry for Holland. Location 12 is also in use, and hence the Finnish entry is placed at the third attempt in location 13. The hash code for the Spanish key is again 11 and, as a result of previous entries, five attempts are necessary before it can be placed in location 15. Finally the addition of Czechoslovakia shows that overflow can occur even when no hash code is repeated; the home base for this record has been used as an overflow area and the record is displaced to location 18.

The difficulty of placing the Spanish entry, in particular, may suggest that hash coding is a poor method of accessing a table, but it should be remembered that all the earlier entries in this table were made at the first attempt, and to create the table as it now stands has required on average only 1.75 attempts per entry. This is not an unreasonable overhead, since each attempt involves only the

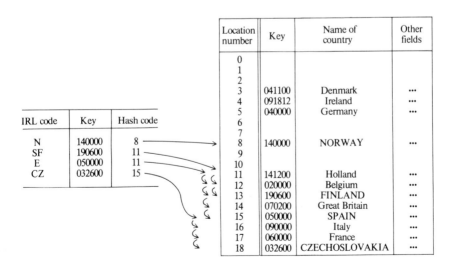

Fig. 6.3   Simple or 'progressive' overflow in a hash-coded table

comparison of the incoming key with the existing key field: if it is empty (simply indicated in this example by a zero key), then the entry can be made; if the keys match then an existing entry is being corrected; otherwise a collision has occurred and the attempt is repeated at the next position of the table (or at position zero if the end of the table has been reached).

Other overflow methods

In avoiding collisions, a critical factor is obviously the size of the space allocated to the table or, more accurately, the proportion of that space which has been occupied. Collisions are more likely to occur as the table fills up – as was seen in the example in Fig. 6.3 – but experiments have shown that in general their frequency increases rapidly only as the table becomes more than about 70 per cent full. To avoid this phenomenon, the space allocated to a hash table should always be at least a third larger than the expected total size of the entries.

A disadvantage of the simple overflow method used in Fig. 6.3 is that it creates 'clusters': when the overflow area for location L is location L + 1 (or, more generally, L + K) then keys which overflow from location L will clash with keys whose hash code is L + K, and thereafter with those whose code is L + 2K etc. This is known as 'primary clustering' and the Spanish entry in Fig. 6.3 was a severe example. The problem can be resolved by using a set of *quadratic* overflow locations, $L + Ki + Ji^2$ ($i = 1,2,3, \ldots$) in place of the linear set $L + Ki$, so that the sequences of overflow locations do not overlap (Fig. 6.4). In either case, the addition is carried out modulo the table size, so that the table is treated as a pseudo-cyclic storage area.

The quadratic method still suffers from 'secondary clustering' because all keys which overflow from location L follow a common set of overflow steps and therefore clash amongst themselves. This can be avoided if the overflow increment,

Linear overflow

Initial location	L	L+K	L+2K
Overflow locations	L+K L+2K L+3K ⋮	L+2K L+3K ⋮	L+3K ⋮

Quadratic overflow

Initial location	L	L+K+J	L+2K+2J	L+2K+4J
Overflow locations	L+K+J L+2K+4J L+3K+9J ⋮	L+2K+2J L+3K+5J ⋮	L+3K+3J ⋮	L+3K+5J ⋮

Fig. 6.4   The use of quadratic overflow to avoid primary clustering in a hash table

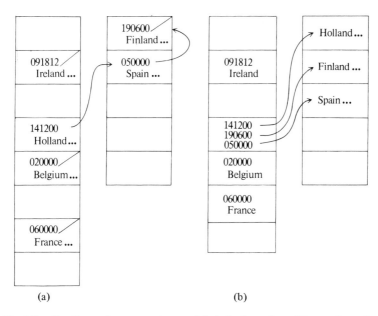

Fig. 6.5   Overflow using a separate area: (a) chained overflow; (b) tagged overflow

as well as the initial hash code, depends on the key which is being entered in the table.

A more fundamental change in policy is to place records which collide in an area separate from the primary table. Such records are stored in the order of their occurrence, so that the overflow area does not contain the gaps which exist in the primary area to minimize collisions. However, each record in the overflow area must be associated with its home base in the primary table, so that it can be retrieved when necessary. To do this, all records whose keys hash to a common value are linked by a chain of pointers to their home base (Fig. 6.5(a)).

The time taken to follow such a chain can be avoided if, once a collision has occurred, the home base in question is made to contain a key and an associated pointer or 'tag' for *every* entry whose key hashes to this base, the tag indicating directly the position of the corresponding record in the overflow area (Fig. 6.5(b)). This is likely to mean that the record previously placed in the home base must itself be relocated so that space is available for the tags to be recorded. Both 'chaining' and 'tagging' attempt to minimize collisions, and thus gain speed of access by separating the primary and overflow areas, but at the cost of additional storage for pointers. Tagging reduces the maximum search length to two steps, but is more complex in operation.

Deletion of entries from a table
Although, hopefully, there will rarely be cause to delete an entry from a table, provision must be made for this operation. The difficulty is greatest when the

table has been created by use of a hash function; in this case an obsolete record cannot simply be replaced by a null record, or its key field returned to an 'empty' value, because this prevents access to any records which have collided at this point and been placed in overflow locations – remember that the access algorithm attempts to follow an overflow chain only if a location is non-empty. Instead, a validity field (which can be a single bit) must be incorporated in each record so that records which are obsolete can be distinguished from those which are live, while either can be distinguished from an unused position whose key field is zero (or some other convenient and distinctive value). If the table is accessed in order to search for a particular entry, obsolete records which are encountered are ignored. If the table is accessed in order to add a new entry, and an obsolete record is encountered, the latter can be overwritten by a record corresponding to the new entry.

When a table has been created by address caculation, each record has its appointed position and an obsolete record can be deleted, i.e. replaced by a null record or key field, without affecting the use of other records in the table in any way.

When a table has been sorted and then stored sequentially, a record can be deleted, provided that the binary search algorithm will ignore empty positions arising in this way – making its comparison instead with an adjacent key field. Both for sorted and for hash-coded tables, the storage should be reconsidered once a number of deletions have occurred, otherwise search operations will become increasingly inefficient in operation.

Examples of algorithms for hash-coded tables*

The procedures ADD, REHASH, and DELETE carry out three standard operations on a hash-coded table. The procedure ADD enters one new element, the procedure REHASH recreates a table completely using a new hash code, and the procedure DELETE discards one element but preserves its position in order to maintain a possible overflow chain. The algorithms use a quadratic overflow method when necessary.

A sequential area is simulated by using the array

REFERENCE(ENTRY) ARRAY TABLE(1 :: SIZE)

to access records of the class

RECORD ENTRY (INTEGER K; STRING(8) S1,S2);

The K-field contains the KEY of each entry and CODE is a suitable function of KEY (e.g. KEY(mod SIZE)) which determines the home position of the entry in TABLE.

---

*These may be omitted at first reading

PROCEDURE ADD(INTEGER VALUE KEY,CODE; STRING(8) VALUE
      Q1,Q2; REFERENCE(ENTRY)ARRAY TABLE(*); INTEGER
      SIZE; LOGICAL U);

COMMENT THIS PROCEDURE ADDS THE DATA (KEY,Q1,Q2) TO
      TABLE (WHICH HAS SIZE SPACES IN ALL) USING THE HASH
      FUNCTION CODE. AN EMPTY SPACE IS INDICATED BY A
      NULL ELEMENT OF TABLE, AND AN ELEMENT WHICH IS
      OBSOLETE AND CAN BE OVERWRITTEN HAS A
      K(KEY) − FIELD VALUE OF ZERO. QUADRATIC OVERFLOW
      IS USED AND 5 ATTEMPTS IN ALL MAY BE MADE TO PLACE
      THE NEW DATA. AFTER THIS THE PROCEDURE IS LEFT WITH
      THE VALUE U = FALSE. IF THE DATA IS SUCCESSFULLY
      PLACED U HAS THE VALUE TRUE;

```
BEGIN INTEGER I,LOC;
     I := 0;
     LOC := CODE + 1:
     WHILE (TABLE(LOC) ¬= NULL) AND (K(TABLE(LOC)) ¬= 0) AND
         (K(TABLE(LOC)) ¬= KEY) DO
         BEGIN
         IF I = 4 THEN BEGIN U := FALSE:
                         WRITE("NO SPACE AFTER 5 ATTEMPTS
                             TO PLACE",KEY);
                         GOTO EXIT
                     END;
         I := I + 1;
          LOC := (CODE + I + I * I)  REM SIZE + 1
          END;
     IF (TABLE(LOC) ¬= NULL) AND (K(TABLE(LOC)) = KEY) THEN
         WRITEON("PREVIOUS ENTRY WITH SAME KEY
         REPLACED");
     TABLE(LOC) := ENTRY(KEY,Q1,Q2);
     U := TRUE;
EXIT:
END ADD;
```

PROCEDURE REHASH (INTEGER KEY,NEWCODE;
      REFERENCE(ENTRY)ARRAY TABLE,NEWTABLE(*); INTEGER
      SIZE,NEWSIZE; LOGICAL V);

COMMENT THIS PROCEDURE RE-STORES THE DATA OF TABLE IN
      NEWTABLE , USING THE HASH FUNCTION NEWCODE. THE
      SIZES OF THE TABLES MAY BE THE SAME OR DIFFERENT.IF

ANY ENTRY IS UNSUCCESSFUL AFTER 5 ATTEMPTS THE
PROCEDURE IS ABANDONED WITH V = FALSE, OTHERWISE
V = TRUE;

```
BEGIN FOR I := 1 UNTIL NEWSIZE DO NEWTABLE(I) := NULL;
      FOR I := 1 UNTIL SIZE DO
            IF TABLE(I) ¬= NULL THEN
            BEGIN
            KEY := K(TABLE(I));
            ADD(KEY,NEWCODE,S1(TABLE(I)),S2(TABLE(I)),NEWTABLE,
                  NEWSIZE,V);
            IF ¬V THEN
                  BEGIN WRITE("REHASH FAILS AFTER 5 ATTEMPTS TO
                        STORE",KEY);
                        GOTO EXIT
                  END
            END;
EXIT:
END REHASH;

   PROCEDURE  DELETE (INTEGER VALUE KEY,CODE;
      REFERENCE(ENTRY)ARRAY TABLE(*); INTEGER SIZE;
      LOGICAL U);

   COMMENT  THIS PROCEDURE WILL INDICATE AN OBSELETE
      ENTRY IN TABLE BY MAKING ITS K(KEY)–FIELD–VALUE
      ZERO. IF THE DATA WHICH HAS BECOME OBSELETE CANNOT
      BE FOUND IN TABLE THEN U IS GIVEN THE VALUE FALSE,
      OTHERWISE U HAS THE VALUE TRUE ON EXIT;

   BEGIN INTEGER I,LOC;
      I := 0;
      LOC := CODE + 1;
      WHILE TABLE(LOC) ¬= NULL DO
      BEGIN IF K(TABLE(LOC)) = KEY THEN
            BEGIN   K(TABLE(LOC)) := 0;
                  U := TRUE;
                  GOTO EXIT
            END;
         IF I < 4 THEN I := I + 1;
         LOC := (CODE + I + I * I) REM SIZE + 1
      END;
      WRITE(I + 1,"POSITIONS EXAMINED BUT NO RECORD FOUND
            WITH KEY",KEY);
      U := FALSE;
   EXIT:
   END DELETE;
```

116

Files

A file may be defined as a set of records all of which relate to a particular area of information, such as a file of vehicle registrations and owners, or a file of components stocked by an electronics manufacturer, or a monthly sales ledger for a business. Some variations may occur in the format of the records contained in a file — in particular, they may vary in length — but the major distinction between a file and a table is that the former term is used to refer to very much larger volumes of data, measured in many millions of characters, and therefore too large to be contained in the main store of a computer system.

The methods used to create storage structures for such large volumes of data are, of course, strongly influenced by the physical characteristics of the devices used for this auxiliary storage. The main memory is a *random-access* store because the time taken to access any location within it is independent of any previous access. By contrast, a magnetic tape is a *serial* store because the only way to move from one item on it to another is to wind the tape steadily from the previous location to the new one (including rewinding, if necessary). Between these extremes, a replaceable magnetic disc unit is a *direct-access* device in which the time taken to reach an item of data does depend on the previous state of the device, but it is possible to move directly to certain areas of the store.

As shown in Fig. 6.6, a replaceable disc unit consists of circular tracks on a number of discs which are rotating at high speed on a common axis. Data are taken to and from the tracks by recording heads (one head per disc surface) which move as a set in and out between the discs, rather like a comb. The time taken to access any location therefore has two components

1 the time to move the heads to the correct track position, and
2 the time for the required location to rotate to the head position.

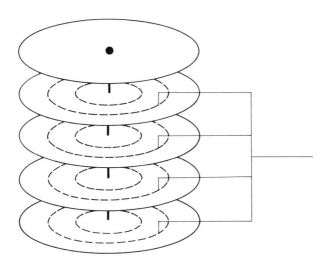

Fig. 6.6   Schematic diagram of a disc pack

117

The former time is very large by comparison with the latter, and this creates the important concept of a *cylinder* or *seek area* of data which can be accessed 'directly', namely all data recorded on the cylinder of tracks determined by the current position of the recording heads.

A disc pack of this type is the most common form of direct- access store, and typically can hold 60 million characters (as compared with approximately 20 million characters on a magnetic tape). A newly developed device designed to give a measure of direct-access even for exceptionally large volumes of data consists of a number of tape cassettes, any one of which can be automatically selected and its contents transferred to a disc unit, whence they can be read 'directly'. In this context the seek area is the cassette, and the device can have nearly 5000 cassettes, holding over 200 000 million characters of data.

Either a magnetic tape or a disc pack can be removed from its drive unit and this means that large off-line 'libraries' can be established from which data are loaded on the computer system only when needed. Valuable security can also be gained by keeping duplicate files of critical data. However, auxiliary storage devices are all slower and less flexible in operation than the main store, and data from a file are therefore transferred to and from a *buffer area* in the main store when processing is necessary. The speed of the transfer can be increased by using two (or more) buffer areas alternately, but the initial time to access the data is critically dependent on the file storage structure which is used on the auxiliary device.

File organization and access

The *organization* of a file refers to the manner in which the constituent records have been arranged on the storage device. The *access method* for a file is the manner in which references are made to the stored data. The same terminology is used for both purposes, but it is important to distinguish the two meanings; the method of access to a file need not necessarily correspond to its organization, though this is generally the case.

Serial storage means that a file is recorded without any organization beyond that imposed by its physical position on the device, and clearly such files can be retrieved only in a similar serial manner. This apart, there are three important methods of ordering a file on the basis of a chosen key field which uniquely distinguishes each record in the file. These methods are

> random,
> sequential, and
> indexed sequential.

Random storage is achieved in the same manner as for tables by applying a hash function to the key of the record and obtaining a storage address. A possible difference is that the address may refer to a storage area (known as a bucket) in which a number of records can be placed rather than to a unique location. The use of a bucket can simplify the problem of handling records of varying lengths and reduce the occurrence of overflow records. Additional time is needed to search within the bucket, where records may be held in an arbitrary order, but this time is small in relation to the time taken to access the bucket itself. In the case of a disc store, the bucket address involves a cylinder number, a track number, and possibly a track sector. If overflow occurs, there is a strong case for using an overflow area on the same cylinder as the 'home' address in order to minimize the re-access time. The disadvantage of this choice is that, instead of having a unique overflow area, space must be set aside for this purpose on every cylinder occupied by the file.

Sequential storage implies that all records in the file are sorted into key order before being stored. When the file is stored on magnetic tape, sequential access is the only possible method of ordered use. The records are arranged in blocks corresponding in size to the buffer area or areas in main store, but a block, once created, cannot be replaced with sufficient accuracy to permit amendments to be made 'in situ' even when the length of the records does not change. Consequently a completely new tape must be written whenever a file on magnetic tape is updated.

When a disc unit is used, more precise forms of sequential access are possible, using address estimation or binary searching techniques as described earlier for tables. It is also possible to update a subsection of a sequential file, such as the contents of a track, provided care is taken to ensure that the sequential ordering is maintained.

Indexed sequential storage is a structure which utilizes the operational characteristics of a direct-access device, and is more flexible in modification than a sequentially stored file. A record is assigned to a bucket determined by its key, but the buckets themselves need not be ordered; instead, an index ordered by key value contains the address of each bucket. (When the bucket holds more than one record, only the largest key is indexed.)

The index is obviously much smaller than the file itself, and part or all of it may be held in the main store. In its simplest form, the index is a one-level table (Fig. 6.7(a)), but for large volumes of data a tree-structured index is frequently used (Fig. 6.7(b)), typically involving a master index, a cylinder index, and a track index for each access to the file. Notice that this technique corresponds to the use of access vectors in the storage of arrays (chapter 2).

When an indexed sequential file is updated, the new or amended record is, if possible, placed in the bucket determined by the value of its key when compared with the indexed values. If there is insufficient space, however, then the record must be placed in an overflow area, and either the index must be re-sorted or a pointer must be placed in the home bucket to link it to the overflow area. The normal indexed sequential method is the latter, so that the indexes remain unchanged but chains of overflow pointers can develop. This solution is simple and efficient in operation so long as overflow records are rare.

The reorganization of a large file as overflow chains become too long would be a major undertaking, and frequent overflow is more likely when the volume

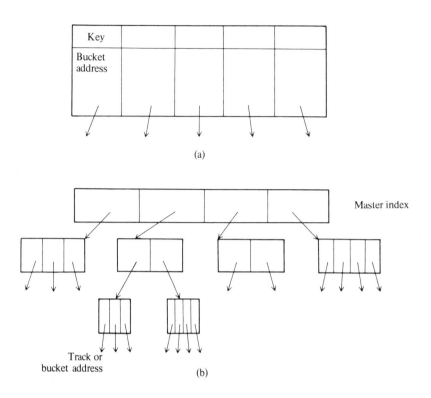

Fig. 6.7 (a) Simple one-level index; (b) three-level index structure

of data is very large and its pattern of development relatively unpredictable —
for example, in a multi-purpose integrated data base. The alternative method of
handling an indexed storage structure and its overflow records has been called
(somewhat misleadingly) a *virtual-storage access method*. It places an overflow
record in a newly defined bucket, for which an entry must be created in the
index structure. (Further overflow at the same point can take its appropriate
place in the new bucket until this too has been filled.) Since a new bucket is
accessed in the same manner as existing buckets, retrieval time is independent of
whether overflow has occurred. The penalty incurred is the need to reorganize
the index structure at the time of overflow, which can involve changes at more
than one level.

The storage organization used for this purpose is somewhat similar to the
provision of space for record structures in the Algol W system (chapter 5). The
master index points to a number of 'pages' or 'control areas', each of which
contains a further index level pointing to buckets or 'control-intervals' within
the page. (A page could be physically implemented as a cylinder, and a bucket as
a track.) Records within a bucket are held in sequential key-order. An important
feature is that, to allow some 'slack' for expansion, the initial allocation of

records does not completely fill any bucket, and some buckets on a page are not used at all.

If overflow occurs, an attempt is first made to find an empty bucket on the current page; if this is successful, the existing records and the newcomer are divided in correct sequence between the old bucket and the new one, and the bucket index for this page is updated. If no empty bucket exists, then a new page is allocated to the file, half the buckets of the old page are copied on to it (the remainder being freed), and the page index of the file is updated. The new record is then added to an appropriate bucket as before.

If the volume of data is small, the standard indexed sequential method will require less space, since it does not allow for 'slack' buckets on a page or cylinder. But as volume and overflow increase, the alternative 'virtual storage' method will not require space for overflow pointers, and when necessary will reorganize the index structure rather than the file as a whole. Notice that it also becomes straightforward to access the entire file sequentially if this is appropriate.

Inverted files

Consider a table of hotel accommodation and assume that it is arranged alphabetically by the name of the hotel (Fig. 6.8). Then a typical enquiry might seek information about (a) a particular hotel, or (b) a hotel in a specified town, or (c) a hotel in a specified town which is small but can offer a lift. Enquiry (a) can be answered by a standard binary search of the table, but the table is unordered in relation to (b) and (c) and, in the absence of any further organization, every entry in the table must be examined to satisfy these requests fully.

Clearly a re-ordering of the table (e.g., by name of town) merely creates an alternative set of problems, and if enquiries based on fields other than the key field are frequent, the only solution is to maintain a subordinate table or index for each of the fields subject to enquiries (Fig. 6.9). These tables are ordered by the attribute concerned, but can refer to records in the main table by their position; thus there is associative access to a subtable followed by direct access

Location	Name of hotel	Town	Size of hotel	Lift
1	Avonside	Bath	Small	No
2	Berkeley	Weston	Small	No
3	Gatehouse	Wells	Small	Yes
4	Grand	Bristol	Large	Yes
5	Imperial	Weston	Large	Yes
6	Queens	Bath	Medium	No
7	Regency	Bath	Medium	Yes
8	Royal	Bristol	Medium	Yes
9	Woodland	Bristol	Small	No

Fig. 6.8   Table of hotel accommodation

Town index		Size index		Lift index	
Bath	1	Large	4	No	1
	6		5		2
	7	Medium	6		6
Bristol	4		7		9
	8		8	Yes	3
	9	Small	1		4
Wells	3		2		5
Weston	2		3		7
	5		9		8

Fig. 6.9   Subordinate indices for Fig. 6.8

to the main table. When an enquiry such as (c) involves more than one attribute, lists of possibilities can be obtained from each subtable, and only those records which are common to all the relevant lists are accessed in the main table. For enquiry (c), using the data of the example, the list of 'small' hotels is (1,2,3,9) and the 'lift' list is (3,4,5,7,8); if the town specified is Wells, record number three (the Gatehouse Hotel) uniquely satisfies the enquiry, but for any other towns the solution set is empty.

A disadvantage of this method is that the number of entries in each section of the subtables is non-uniform, making any specific attribute value in a subtable more difficult to locate (e.g., the value 'small' in the size index). A further problem is to maintain the ordering of the table and each subtable if the set of records is subject to change. In an alternative method, considered by Vose and Richardson (1972) and by Inglis (1974), a sequential index number (SIN) is generated for each record as it is created, and a basic index is maintained in SIN order containing the key of each record and a set of pointers, one for each class of attributes which may be referenced, which link records having a common value within each attribute (Fig. 6.10). In addition to the basic index, there is an index for each attribute, held in alphabetic or numeric order of value within attribute, and containing attribute value, the latest SIN having this value, and the length of chain for this value (i.e., the number of records having this attribute value). Besides the indices, the set of records which form the table is stored as before, ordered by hotel name, and containing fields such as hotel address which will not be the subject of an initial enquiry.

In this system enquiry (a) is answered by accessing the table in the standard way. To answer (b), look in the town index for (say) Bristol; this indicates SIN = 6 in the basic index, and hence the key name 'Royal', while the town field of this entry leads to the further entries whose SIN values are five and one, corresponding to the key names 'Woodland' and 'Grand'. These three key names can now be used to access the complete records in the table. Enquiry (c) is answered in a similar way by accessing first the appropriate values in the town, size, and lift indices; thereafter the shortest of the three possible chains indicates a 'short-list' of possible SIN values in the basic index.

Basic index SIN		Key	Town	Size	Lift
1		Grand	✓	✓	✓
2		Berkeley	✓	✓	✓
3		Gatehouse	✓	2	1
4		Queens	✓	✓	2
5		Woodland	1	3	4
6		Royal	5	4	3
7		Regency	4	6	6
8		Avonside	7	5	5
9		Imperial	2	1	7

Town index

Attribute value	Latest SIN	Length
Bath	8	3
Bristol	6	3
Wells	3	1
Weston	9	2

Size index

Attribute value	Latest SIN	Length
Large	9	2
Medium	7	3
Small	8	4

Lift index

Attribute value	Latest SIN	Length
No	8	4
Yes	9	5

Fig. 6.10   Inverted file structure using multiple links

By comparison with the previous method, this alternative requires additional space for the basic index, but the sub-indices are smaller and of fixed size. It is significantly easier to accommodate new entries: besides placing a record in the table itself, an entry is added sequentially to the basic index, and in each attribute index the 'latest SIN' and 'length' fields of the appropriate value are updated. Notice that there is no need to re-order any of these indices, as would be the case in the method discussed first. As an example, suppose that the Park Hotel, a small hotel in Bristol which has a lift, is to be added to the data: the steps would be

1   generate the SIN value 10,
2   change the Bristol entry in the town index to 'Bristol,10,4',
3   make similar changes in the other sub-indices,
4   add the entry 'Park, 6,8,9' to the basic index, which is otherwise unaltered.

If, conversely, entries in the table become obsolete, they must be marked as such rather than deleted, so that the chains of pointers on which the retrieval of other records depends are not destroyed (cf. overflow in hash-coded tables). Similarly if a field value of a record changes (e.g., a hotel instals a lift) the previous record must be marked as obsolete and a new record created to replace it; this can lead to a serious penalty in storage space if amendments are frequent.

Inverted access to a set of data is of principal importance when the set is a large file held on auxiliary storage rather than a table which can be held wholly in main store; for many large problems, the indices themselves may have to be kept on auxiliary storage. When adding new entries, the second of the two methods described above is the more efficient, because no reorganization is necessary and time-consuming accesses to auxiliary storage are therefore minimized. In retrieval operations, a chain must be followed in the basic index to obtain the addresses of all records having a stipulated attribute value, and each step of the chain may require a separate device access. By comparison, the first method must locate the relevant section (e.g., small hotels) within a sub-index in which the sections are of varying length but, once found, the addresses of the corresponding records are grouped together.

Problems

6.1 Explain what is meant by a 'table' and describe carefully three different methods of accessing this type of structure. State, with reasons, which method you would use in order to access the following data held in a computer store:

(a) a table of share prices on the Stock Exchange
(b) an index of names held by an employment agency.

6.2 Create two arrays of 1000 locations each and use a random number generator to produce N integer code values in the range 0–999. Store the integers in each of the arrays, attempting to place an integer I in location I, but (when necessary) using a linear overflow method in one array and a quadratic method in the other. Count the number of times the overflow algorithm is used in each case and print a table showing the ratios of these values to N for values of N between 400 and 800.

6.3 What are the desirable properties of a hashing function?

A catalogue contains about 500 entries and the total range of catalogue numbers is 100–1400. The numbers were allocated consecutively for entries of the same general kind, the first of a group usually ending in 00. Suggest a suitable hashing function if there is memory available for about 1000 entries.

(Glasgow, 1974)

6.4 Define the terms 'seek area', 'bucket', 'buffer' in relation to files. What connection, if any, exists between the last two of these?

Describe the following:

sequential access method
indexed sequential access method
virtual storage access method

and indicate the file characteristics for which each method is most suitable.

6.5 The data in a student file system contain the following fields: Name – 20 characters, Age – 2 digits, Course – 2 characters, Year – 1 digit, Reference number – 6 digits.

You are required to design a data structure and storage scheme so that the following processes can be achieved:

> add new entries to file;
> remove to another file all entries on a given course or all entries on a given year;
> list all students on a given course and year;
> compute the average age of students on file.

Give any reasons why you consider your choice better than other possible methods.

(Leicester Polytechnic, B.Sc. Comp.Sc, 1974)

6.6 The Ruritanian Telecommunications Department is doing a feasibility study of a project to make telephone directories available on-line. The data to be held include name, address, and telephone number for each subscriber. Two main types of access to the data are envisaged:

(a)   given the name, return the address and telephone number;
(b)   given the telephone number, return the name and address.

Suggest a method of organizing the data and describe how the two types of access would be effected. You should take into account the need to update the data.

Would your method of organization be suitable for the construction of printed area telephone directories listing in name order all the numbers in a given group of exchanges? Explain your answer.

(Glasgow, 1973)

6.7 A lending library wishes to keep in a small computer an index of its books arranged by subject according to the Dewey decimal classification system. It wishes to be able, given a classification number, to access rapidly the entries of all books with that number and with all longer numbers (i.e., books in sub-classification). It also wishes to be able to rapidly add and delete books from its lists, given their classification number. Suggest a suitable data structure, and give appropriate algorithms for (a) printing out a list of all books under a given classification, together with their classification number, and (b) inserting a new book entry into the library.

(Assume that all relevant information about a book can be stored in four computer words, that a pointer can be stored in half a word, with a spare bit left over, and that a standard subroutine PRINTBOOK exists which, given a book entry, prints out the information in a standard format.)

In order to protect itself against fire, etc., the library wishes to dump a complete list of all books, in classification order, onto a magnetic tape once a week. Suggest how this might be done in such a way that your data structure could be easily rebuilt by reading the tape.

(Essex, 1973)

7. Programming languages and data structures

In order to process any given set of data, it is necessary to choose a representation of the data (a storage structure), to provide an algorithm for accessing the chosen structure, and to have means of describing operations on and transformations of the structure. These facilities are provided, to a greater or lesser degree, by the programming languages available to computer users. The extent and sophistication of these features is not, of course, the only criterion in the design and evaluation of a language — other important considerations include simplicity of use, the ease and efficiency of compilation, and the special characteristics of any applications area for which the language is specifically intended. The earlier programming languages in particular gave little scope for varied and flexible data structures, reflecting the origins of the computer as a numerical calculator rather than an information-processing device.

The following descriptions refer to some well-established languages and to others less well known, to some general-purpose languages and to others which are restricted in their objective, but in every case the emphasis is concentrated on those aspects of the language which are particularly relevant to the processing of structures.

Fortran and Cobol

These two languages can reasonably be regarded as the original general-purpose languages for scientific and commercial applications respectively, although both have been substantially modified and extended since their first introduction.

The only type of structure provided by *Fortran* is the array, defined by a DIMENSION statement such as

DIMENSION FORCE (10,5)

which sets up a sequential area in which (say) the air resistance of ten objects at five different speeds can then be recorded. Fortran, unlike Algol, is not a block-structured language, so that once some space has been earmarked in this way it is reserved throughout the program concerned. However, this space may be made to serve a dual role by the use of an EQUIVALENCE statement, which allows two different variables to access the same storage area. For example we may have the vectors defined by

DIMENSION V(50), W(10)

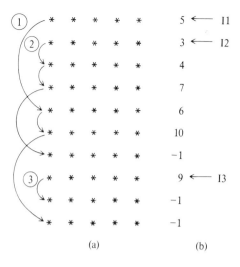

Fig. 7.1   Use of a vector to represent three simple lists

and by writing

EQUIVALENCE (FORCE,V)

the vector V will occupy the same area as the array FORCE. In the same way, writing

EQUIVALENCE (FORCE(1,5),W(1))

will cause W(1) to refer to the same location as FORCE(1,5) and hence, assuming that Fortran arrays are stored column by column, the vector W as a whole will occupy the same set of locations as the fifth and last column of the array FORCE.

Similarly, a single column vector can be used to store a number of disjoint single lists. Suppose the objects measured for air resistance fall into three categories as shown by the links in Fig. 7.1(a). Then we can define three vectors C1, C2, C3 which share a common space by writing

INTEGER C1(10), C2(10), C3(10)
EQUIVALENCE (C1, C2, C3)

and set up the values shown in Fig. 7.1(b); the initial positions of the lists are held in scalar locations I1, I2, I3, but each chain is continued in the common vector until the special value -1 is reached. For this method to be used, it is not necessary for the lists to be disjoint, but they must be simple, i.e., common sublists may be represented, but not branch points, for which an additional field or dimension is required.

Cobol was the first language to make a conscious distinction between the structure of data and the operations to be carried out upon it, by introducing a

```
01   TRAFFIC
     02   PLACE
          04   TOWN
          04   ROAD
     02   DATE
          03   CAR
          03   BUS
          03   TRUCK
```

Fig. 7.2

Data Division and a Procedure Division as separate though related parts of a program, together with an Environment Division to achieve machine independence for the descriptions. Data are organized as a set of logical *records*, each of which can be subdivided in a hierarchical manner to yield elementary items or groups at subordinate *levels*, the levels being indicated by numbers of increasing (though not necessarily consecutive) values. Figure 7.2 shows the structure of a typical record for a traffic survey, omitting the details of format for the elementary items such as TOWN and CAR.

This hierarchical mode of definition means that all data structures in Cobol have the basic form of a tree, but any item below the root level can be given the form of a vector by using the OCCURS option. Suppose that data are collected on five days and that trucks are recorded in three classes according to weight. Then the new record description is shown in Fig. 7.3, and the data structure is a combination of a tree and a table. The number of light trucks recorded on the fourth day can be written TRUCK (4,1); more generally, if DAY is an integer variable which can take any value from 1 to 5, the number of light trucks on any one DAY is TRUCK (DAY, 1).

In this way, some quite complex structures can be set up in Cobol, and there are also powerful file-handling and input—output facilities, as should be expected in a language designed to handle large quantities of alphanumeric information from a commercial environment. However, the structures are not dynamically variable — only their contents can alter — and there is no provision for data relationships other than those which are tabular or hierarchical.

PL/1

Work on PL/1 developed in the period 1963—5 as an attempt to design a unified high-level language having the widest possible applicability, drawing on

```
01   TRAFFIC
     02   PLACE
          04   TOWN
          04   ROAD
     02   DATE OCCURS 5 TIMES
          03   CAR
          03   BUS
          03   TRUCK OCCURS 3 TIMES
```

Fig. 7.3

128

experience of the established languages at that time – particularly Fortran, Cobol, and Algol. To assist its all-purpose aims, a very wide variety of data types is available, and for the representation of relationships these include arrays (which may have either fixed or dynamically variable bounds), hierarchical structures as in Cobol, and the ability to construct dynamically linked structures as in Algol W.

Like Algol, and unlike Fortran, PL/1 is a block-structured language: that is to say that a program consists of nested sub-units. Each sub-unit or *block* provides a natural basis for the allocation of storage, which can be released when execution of the block is completed, so that at any stage in its execution a program need claim no more storage than is necessary for that stage. PL/1 takes advantage of this but, true to its philosophy, also allows the user to control storage allocation in other ways if his program requires this.

There are four possible choices – AUTOMATIC, STATIC, CONTROLLED, or BASED – and the method to be used is in general specified in a DECLARE statement which defines the type and format of a variable. STATIC storage specifies that space is assigned throughout the execution of the program, as in Fortran. AUTOMATIC storage means that the block structure is used to control the 'scope' (or availability) of a variable, which can be accessed in, and only in, the block where it is declared (including any inner block, provided the variable is not redefined there). If no instruction is given to the contrary, AUTOMATIC storage is adopted by default.

CONTROLLED storage places the onus on the user to ALLOCATE and FREE the necessary space explicitly as and when required. An important feature of CONTROLLED storage is that it can operate as a stack: given the following skeleton program

```
        DECLARE S CONTROLLED;
        .
        .
        .
L1:     ALLOCATE S;
        .
        .
        .
L2:     ALLOCATE S;
        .
        .
        .
L3:     FREE S;
        .
        .
        .
L4:     FREE S;
```

```
DECLARE     1   ELEMENT BASED (FIRST);
            2     DATUM CHARACTER (1);
            2     LINK POINTER;
ALLOCATE ELEMENT;
DATUM = 'A';
LINK = NULL;
```

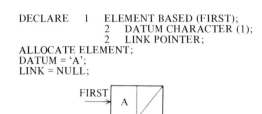

Fig. 7.4   BASED storage

space is generated by the statement L1 for the variable S, and statement L2
generates further space for a distinct variable whose name is also S; at this point
the previous meaning and value of S are suspended (but not lost) and only the
new variable is valid until statement L3 is reached; the space for the second
realization of S is then given up and the former value regained until it too is
released by statement L4. Thus a series of values can be 'stacked' in successive
realizations of S.

When BASED storage is used, the declaration of the variable defines the
format of an item of data, the space for an *instance* of the variable is created by
an ALLOCATE statement, and the location of this space is indicated by a
POINTER variable which is specified in the definition of the BASED variable.
For example, the statements in Fig. 7.4 set up a simple item called ELEMENT
referenced by the variable FIRST and containing two fields called DATUM and
LINK whose values are 'A' and NULL respectively. FIRST is defined by context
as a POINTER variable, and since assignment is made without qualification to
DATUM and LINK it is implied that the pointer in the declaration is to be used
as the base for their access. Notice the assignment symbol '=' as in Fortran, the
similarity to Cobol in defining the format of the data item, and the use of NULL
as in Algol W.

Another pointer variable, P, can be introduced and used to indicate a new
instance of ELEMENT by means of the statements

DECLARE P POINTER;
ALLOCATE ELEMENT SET(P);

where the use of SET(P) for this allocation ensures that the pointer FIRST still
indicates the previous structure (Fig. 7.5(a)). The two elements can then be
linked in order of their creation (Fig. 7.5(b)) by the assignment statement

LINK = P

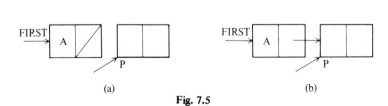

(a)   (b)

Fig. 7.5

To terminate this short list, it is necessary to refer to the LINK field of the second item, which is not based on the pointer used in the declaration of ELEMENT. The reference must therefore be qualified by writing P $->$ LINK, and the assignment statement is

P $->$ LINK = NULL

which can be read as 'P points to an element whose LINK field becomes NULL'. Similarly the DATUM field is given the value 'B' by the statement

P $->$ DATUM = 'B'

This 'concatenated' notation – first find P, then the stated field of the appropriate element – is consistent with the fully qualified name ELEMENT.LINK which is used in PL/1 (as in Cobol) for the LINK field in the ELEMENT structure, but it contrasts with the functional notation of Algol W where, in similar circumstances, the statements would be LINK(P) := NULL and DATUM(P) := "B".

These basic operations show that PL/1, like Algol W, enables the user to define heterogeneous data items (confusingly termed structures in PL/1) and set up links between them at run time to represent structures (in the more general sense used in this book) with dynamic relationships. However, there are a number of differences between POINTER/BASED structures and REFERENCE/RECORD classes. The declaration of a BASED structure defines by context a base pointer, but POINTER variables are not restricted to a specified set or sets of structures. This gives greater flexibility to the user, but greater risk of setting up inappropriate links between logically unrelated structures.

A record in Algol W is merely a sequence of 'simple types' whereas an item (structure) in PL/1 can have a hierarchical format. This simplifies the representation of information like that of Fig. 7.6, while still allowing instances of 'STUDENT' to be linked dynamically by, say, name of 'DEGREE'. Hierarchical format is also of value in enabling a subset of the data to be referenced as a whole; for example, if RESULT is a variable having the same structure as the subset COURSE, the aggregate statement

RESULT = COURSE (1)

will assign the values of TITLE and MARK field by field.

STUDENT							
NAME		DEGREE	COURSE 1		COURSE 2		...	COURSE n	
SURNAME	INITIALS		TITLE	MARK	TITLE	MARK		TITLE	MARK

Fig. 7.6

Space allocation for BASED variables is controlled by the user, and hence he must not only claim space for an element by the ALLOCATE statement, but also release it when appropriate by using a FREE statement such as

FREE P –> ELEMENT, ELEMENT

After this statement neither P nor FIRST has a meaningful value. Notice that pointers do not revert to any previous values they may have had and, for example, in order to release only the first of a linked set of ELEMENTs, the user must be careful to preserve a distinct pointer to the remainder of the set:

P = LINK
FREE ELEMENT
FIRST = P

However, provided suitable pointers are maintained, any current instance of a BASED variable can be accessed, whereas only the most recent instance of a CONTROLLED variable is available.

The operation of the FREE statement places two burdens on the user: to determine when an item is no longer required by *any* part of a complex structure, and conversely to ensure that he does not remove all pointers to a redundant BASED variable without first using a FREE statement to make the space available for further use. Note, by contrast, that these are the problems which led to the use of a garbage collector and automatic free store maintenance in Algol W systems.

Despite the vast range of possible applications, PL/1 does not allow the user to extend the syntax and add features to his own design and needs. Instead it makes an ambitious attempt to include sufficient features and attributes to gain wide acceptance. As a result it is a very large language — some would say clumsy — both to use and to implement, but it does try to shield the user from the need to master details which are unimportant in a particular application (e.g., storage allocation or type conversion) by allowing the most common modes of use to be gained by default. The facilities it provides for processing dynamic structures are very general and unsophisticated and this is not, perhaps, the easiest area of the language to use, but it was the first major general-purpose language to have such features incorporated in its design rather than added as a package of specialized procedures.

Pascal

Pascal (Wirth, 1972) is a general-purpose language which, in contrast to PL/1, is concise and has a clearly defined syntax. Its design is based on Algol 60 and Algol W but neither language is a subset of Pascal.

Data types in Pascal are classed as 'simple', 'structured', or 'pointer', and a valuable distinction is made between the *definition of a data type* and the *declaration of a variable* to hold a value of a stated type. A type definition is written

    type ⟨type identifier⟩ = ⟨data type⟩

where ⟨type identifier⟩ is a name for the type which is being defined, and ⟨data type⟩ determines the range of values for this type.

    This may be confusing when stated in such general terms, but the distinction between a type definition and a variable declaration can be illustrated by considering a variable of **scalar** type, which is a simple type consisting of a stated set of items. Suppose that v is a variable which may take as its value any one of the letters a, e, i, o, u; then the scalar data type 'vowel' can be defined as

    type vowel = (a,e,i,o,u)

and followed by the variable declaration:

    var v : vowel

Similarly a data type 'season' can be declared as

    type season = (spring, summer, autumn, winter)

A shortened syntax is also permissible, in which a type definition is implied merely by declaring

    var v : (a,e,i,o,u)

    Four sets of items are so common that they are given standard scalar names and taken to have a global definition. These are the integers, real numbers, Booleans, and characters, so that the declaration of integer variables i and j, a real variable x, and a character variable s, can be written in the shortened syntax as

    var   i,j : integer;

           x : real;

           s : char;

    Except in the case of the Booleans, **true** and **false**, the precise range of each standard scalar type is implementation dependent. However, variables can be restricted to a 'subrange' of a scalar type by stating a lower and upper bound within the range. This is interpreted with reference to the order of definition if the scalar type is defined explicitly, or in numeric or collating order when taking a subrange of a standard set. For example,

var k : 0 .. 9	k is a one-digit integer
var z : -1.0 .. 1.0	$\|z\| \leqslant 1$
var growth : spring .. autumn	'growth' has three possible values.

    Structured data in Pascal can take one of four basic types — file, set, array, or record. A **file** type is a structure containing a sequence of elements all of the same type, for example,

    var f : **file of** char

Its length is not defined initially and new elements must be added at the end of the file. Only one element of the file f, determined by the current read/write head position, can be accessed at any one time. This is done through a buffer indicated by the variable f↑, which is automatically declared at the same time as the file f.

    A **set** type is the set of all subsets of a scalar type. For example, if the scalar type 'coin' is defined as

    type coin = (0.5, 1, 2, 2.5, 5, 10, 50)

and the variable 'change' is declared as

    var change : **set of** coin

then 'change' may take a value which is any one of 2^7 sets (including the empty set) which can be formed from 'coin'. Operations on set types can form their union, intersection, or difference, and membership of a set can be tested by the operator **in**. For example,

    (1, 2) **in** change   has the value **true**

but

    (1, 20) **in** change   has the value **false**

    An **array** is the familiar structure containing a fixed number of elements of homogeneous type which can be accessed by a computable formula or index. For example,

    var a : **array** [1 .. 5, 1 .. 4] **of** real
    var seed : **array** [1 .. 20] **of** season

Notice how the concept of a subrange serves naturally for the bounds of the array. Unlike most recent languages, the authors of Pascal insisted that the bounds should be fixed at compile time in order to make implementation more efficient. The elements of an array are required to be 'homogeneous', i.e., they must have a common data type, but this can be a 'record' (see below) which may contain fields of varied types. As a result, an array in Pascal can take a much more general form than arrays in Algol W or PL/1 and, indeed, more general than the formal definition of an array given earlier in this book.

    A **record** in Pascal is very similar to the structure of the same name in Algol W, but it has been extended in two ways: any component of a record may itself be of structured type, and the final component may have several variants — that is, at any time the value of such a component may be any

134

one of several types, the current type being determined from a 'case list' by the value of a tag field associated with the component. For example,

```
type student = record name: array [1 .. 12] of char;
                      age: integer;
                      married: boolean;
              case   entry: degree of
                            honours: (courseno, class : integer);
                            ordinary: (mark : real)
              end
```

where 'degree' is a scalar type and 'entry' is a variable of type degree which may have the value 'honours' or 'ordinary'.

Besides distinguishing between a type definition and a variable declaration, Pascal is also precise in describing its mode of storage allocation. Data definitions and explicit declarations of variables can be made at the beginning of a program so that they have global scope (i.e, validity throughout the program), or as part of a procedure declaration in which case their scope is local to the procedure. (The symbols **begin** and **end** which are used in Algol also occur in Pascal, but only as brackets for a group of statements; they may not include declarations.) The variables in explicit declarations are said to be 'static' and can be allocated space at compile time.

However, it has been shown that an essential feature of structural processing is the ability to create new elements at run time. Therefore, in addition, at any time during the execution of the program, an element of any valid data type can be created by using a standard procedure 'new (⟨type⟩)' which allocates the necessary space from a free list. No such element, or 'dynamic variable', can be referred to by name (since none has been declared for it) and instead access is by means of a variable of pointer type which is assigned the address of the element newly created by the procedure 'new'. Pointers are restricted to the empty value **nil** or to a specified data type by the notation

↑⟨data type⟩.

They can only be assigned values or tested for equality. For example, having defined the data type 'student' as a record, the declaration

s1, s2: ↑student

creates two pointer variables which can access instances of this type. The procedure statement

new(s1)

then creates such an instance and assigns to the variable 's1' a pointer to its location. If required, a second pointer can be assigned by the statement

s2 := s1

Notice carefully the difference between 's1', which is a variable of type pointer having a value to be interpreted as an address, and 's1↑', which is the variable of type student pointed to by 's1'. Thus 's1↑. age' has an integer value which is the age of the student to which 's1' is pointing.

Dynamic variables of any type can be created in this way, though the procedure is normally confined to records. Since any field of a record can be of pointer type, there is a full structuring capability similar to that of record classes in Algol W. The facility in Algol W of using ambiguous references does not exist in Pascal, but is largely replaced by the ability to define a variant field within a record type.

Two important considerations in the design of Pascal were that it should be easy to teach and learn, and efficient in implementation. Experience has shown that both of these have been achieved in large measure, but the language is not merely a pedagogical device but a practical and powerful tool for the description and solution of a wide range of problems where the structural relationships of data are important. In particular, it has proved of value for system software, where high-level programming languages have so far been little used.

Lisp

Lisp (McCarthy,1960) was designed, and is of practical value, only for problems which are principally concerned with list or symbol processing. It has a highly recursive structure, and one of many unique features is that programs and data share a common format, so that its data structures cannot be described separately from the language.

Notation

Only two types of data are allowed: an *atom*, which is a string of alphanumeric characters, and an *S-expression* (a 'symbolic-expression') which either is an atom or has the form:

⟨⟨S-expression⟩ . ⟨S-expression⟩⟩

for example,

A   (A.B)   (A.(B.C))

This recursive definition allows complex data values to be formed, each of which has the structure of a binary tree (Fig. 7.7).

There is one special atom, NIL, which corresponds to an empty or non-existent branch of a tree. An S-expression of the form

(B.NIL)

is curtailed to simply (B), and furthermore

(A.(B.NIL))

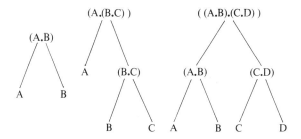

Fig. 7.7   The structure of typical S-expressions in Lisp

is curtailed to

(A,B)

Data which can be expressed in this 'shorthand' form can be represented diagrammatically as a list (Fig. 7.8) which can itself be non-linear. Although the basic 'dot' notation can be invoked if necessary, the more convenient 'list' notation is used in practice in all Lisp programming.

Basic functions of Lisp
A Lisp program consists of a function which is applied to suitable arguments, but each argument can itself be a function, which must first be evaluated; this

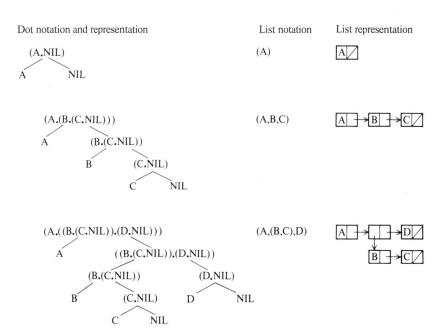

Fig. 7.8   Examples of Lisp data in 'dot' and 'list' notation

137

recursive evaluation can continue to any depth until a function is reached all of whose arguments are constants. Thus, in Lisp, both program and data are recursive. This is not the only point of similarity: the method of evaluation described above shows that any function can also be the *data* for another function; consequently all functions must be written in the same dot or list notation as data; that is,

(FUNCTION, ARG1, ARG2, . . .)

(A meta-language or reference-language also exists, but programs written in it must be converted to dot or list format before execution. To avoid confusion only the latter forms will be used here.)

Lisp contains five elementary functions:

CAR obtains the first element of a list, but is undefined for an atom;
CDR obtains the remainder of a list, but is undefined for an atom;
CONS combines two S-expressions to form a new S-expression;
ATOM has the value true (T) if its argument is an atom, and otherwise false (NIL);
EQ is defined only for atomic arguments, is true if they are the same, and otherwise false.

(The names CAR and CDR are a legacy of the hardware used for the first implementation of Lisp; these names are sometimes replaced by HEAD and TAIL respectively.)

Examples   Suppose that X,Y,Z are variables whose values are (A,B,C), D, and (D,E) respectively. (The manner in which a variable is associated with its value will be described later.) Then,

(CAR,X)	→ A
(CAR,Y)	is undefined
(CDR,X)	→ (B,C)
(CDR,(CDR,X))	→(C)
(CAR,(CDR,(CDR,X)))	→ C
(CONS,Y,NIL)	→ (D)
(CONS,Y,Z)	→ (D,D,E)
(ATOM,X)	→ NIL
(ATOM,Y)	→ T
(EQ,Y,(CAR,Z))	→ T
(EQ,Y,(CDR,Z))	is undefined

In these examples, it is important to notice again that each argument of a function is itself evaluated. It is tempting to believe that (CAR,(A,B,C)) should have the value A, but this is wrong; the system would first attempt to evaluate the argument (A,B,C) by treating A as a function name with B and C as its arguments. The expected result can, however, be achieved by introducing the 'pseudo-function' QUOTE, which has one argument which is also its result — i.e., QUOTE acts as though inhibiting the usual evaluation process. Thus,

(QUOTE,A)   → A
(QUOTE,(A,B,C))   → (A,B,C)
(CAR,(QUOTE,(A,B,C))) → A

If a function has two or more arguments which are to be used without evaluation, QUOTE must be applied to each one. Hence

(CONS, (QUOTE,A,B))

is incorrect syntax: QUOTE has two arguments and CONS has one — the reverse of the correct situation, which is

(CONS,(QUOTE,A),(QUOTE,B))

The result is (A.B) and on this occasion the dot notation is unavoidable.

A choice in the path of execution can be made by using a conditional function which is a concise extension of the **if** . . . **then** . . . **else** construction of Algol. It has the form

(COND,(P1,E1),(P2,E2), . . .)

where Pi are predicates (such as EQ) whose values are T or NIL, and Ei are expressions. The result or value of the entire function is the value of the first Ei for which Pi is true; the atom T can be used as a catch-all predicate whose value is always true. For example, given the variable V, suppose that the result is to be

NIL if the value of V is an atom;
or the head of the list if V is a list of one element only;
or the tail of the list if V is a list of more than one element.

Using the predicate NULL, which is true if and only if its argument has the value NIL, the necessary conditional expression is:

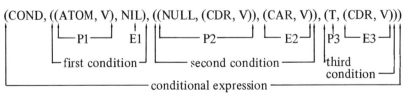

λ-definition of new functions
Suppose that a new list is to be formed by taking the CAR or head of one list and linking it to the CDR or tail of another. Using 'formal parameters' U and V the function might be written as

(CONS, (CAR,V),(CDR,U))

but Lisp (quite properly) insists that this is not precise: if the function is applied to actual parameters X and Y, in which order do X and Y correspond to U and V? Is it by alphabetical order or by order of occurrence in the definition? The ambiguity can be removed if the formal parameters are stated in an explicit order prior to the 'form' of the definition. This is one of the principles of the 'λ-calculus', a formal system of function evaluation, in which the definition of a function is called a 'λ-expression'. A simple example of a λ-expression is

$$\lambda\, i : i^2$$

which can be read as 'the function of i that maps i to i^2'. The corresponding expression in Lisp notation is

(LAMBDA, I, I∗I)

or, more generally,

(LAMBDA, list of formal parameters, form of definition).

Once defined, a lambda expression is a function which can be used just like any other function in the form

(function, arg1, arg2, . . .)

so that

((LAMBDA, I,I∗I), 3)

has the value 9 ('QUOTE' is not required for numbers).

The function considered at the beginning of the last paragraph can now be defined as the lambda-expression

(LAMBDA,(U,V), (CONS,(CAR,V), (CDR,U)))

If the variables X and Z have the same values as before, the result of applying this function is

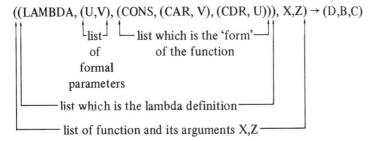

Recursive functions

The importance of recursion in Lisp has already been stressed, and it is often necessary for a function to call itself recursively; for example, the last element of a list V can be found in this way by a function SEEK such that

$$(\text{SEEK,V}) = \begin{cases} (\text{CAR, V}) \text{ if V has only one element, i.e. } (\text{CDR, V}) = \text{NIL} \\ \text{otherwise evaluate } (\text{SEEK,(CDR, V)}). \end{cases}$$

However a lambda-expression is insufficient to describe a recursive function of this kind because it attaches no name to the function which it defines. In order to make effective use of a λ-defined function it is necessary to create one further level of structure in which the special symbol LABEL binds a name to the λ-expression. The format, which again has the standard pattern, is

(LABEL, function name, lambda definition)

and in particular the definition of the function SEEK is

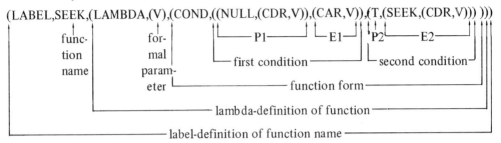

Finally, to apply the function SEEK to the variable Z, the Lisp expression is:

$$((LABEL, SEEK,(LAMBDA,(V), \ldots (CDR,V)))))), Z) \rightarrow E$$

with "function name" labelling the initial portion and "argument" labelling Z.

The object of a recursive program structure is to allow a variable to be used at several levels, making available its value at the current level and preserving any previous value acquired at an 'upper' level. Conversely, a consequence of such a structure is that the name of a function cannot be valid above the level at which it is defined. This means that the function SEEK, for example, can only be used within its own definition — and is 'temporary' rather than 'permanent' or global to a program. In practice, this apparent restriction is not serious, except for mutually recursive functions, as a recursive structure will develop naturally as a function is defined.

The language can be extended indefinitely in this way, but for efficiency Lisp contains a considerable number of built-in functions which have a global 'value' or meaning. Built-in functions, and other constants of the system, are each attached directly to a 'property list' so that a reference to the function name immediately yields its value. By contrast, temporary bindings of a variable and a value during evaluation of a function are all placed on an 'association list' which is pushed down or popped up as bindings are created or deleted. A LABEL-defined function name, being a temporary variable, is placed on the association list together with its λ-expression, and use of the latter may lead to further associations for which a search must be made in the list. Thus the use of the association list, while providing an invaluable form of dynamic storage for a highly recursive language, can be very time-consuming, particularly if it contains many local variables.

141

To gain the advantages of a property list, the user can create further globally defined functions by using DEFINE, which takes the form

(DEFINE,((fname1, λdefn1), (fname2, λdefn2), . . .))

These new functions will be executed just as though they were system-defined functions, and it is this feature which gives Lisp a significant degree of extensibility.

The disadvantages of Lisp are obvious enough: it has only two data types, its recursive notation is very difficult to read, its proliferation of parentheses is sufficient to drive the most careful user to distraction and frequent mistakes, it cannot be regarded as a general-purpose language, and in many implementations of the language its execution is very slow. Yet despite all these faults it has had enthusiastic groups of supporters. A Lisp program is very concise, and in principle is not difficult to write once some experience has been gained with the unfamiliar functional notation and its recursive evaluation. New functions can be defined very easily and the language has been extensively used for heuristic problems, e.g. artificial intelligence and the simulation of games, and for applications which involve symbol processing such as formal algebra and theorem proving. Whatever its practical success, Lisp has been of value for provoking consideration of a radically different form of programming, nor should it be forgotten that the complex dynamic changes in its program structure during execution caused the development (and naming) of garbage collection, now such a widespread technique.

POP2

Experience with Lisp is reflected in the design of POP2, a language created primarily for non-numerical applications and intended for on-line interactive use (the only language of this kind amongst those discussed in this chapter). However, the restricted and confusing syntax of Lisp is replaced by a notation more similar to Algol, and more general data structures are allowed.

In POP2 the name of a variable must be declared, but it is not restricted to any particular type or 'item' of data, thus simplifying incremental compilation of the program. The only 'simple items' used in POP2 are integers and real numbers (logical values are represented by 0 and 1) but there are a number of standard compound items such as lists and arrays, together with provision for the user to define other structures (and operations on them) to suit a particular application. Space for all compound structures, whether standard or not, is made available by an automatic, system-maintained, allocation scheme which invokes a garbage collector as and when necessary.

A *list* is an ordered sequence of items and, since an item may be compound, sublists can occur. A list of specific items is enclosed in square brackets:

[red white blue] —> f
[[scarlet crimson] white blue] —> g

The elements of a list may also be obtained by evaluating expressions, in which case 'decorated brackets' are used:

[% f, "black", n+1 %] —> h

Two lists may be joined as one by the operator '<>' while the functions 'hd' and 'tl' (cf. CAR and CDR), 'cons' (also written '::'), and 'null' all act as in Lisp.

Output is obtained by using the print arrow '=>' after an expression, and is preceded by two asterisks. For example,

f <> [green] =>
** [red white blue green]

hd(g) =>
**[scarlet crimson]

"green" :: nil =>
** [green]

"green" :: f =>
** [green red white blue]

The first of these examples can be generalized by defining a function to add any item z at the end of any list p. The definition is:

function append z p; p <> [z::nil] **end**;

where **function** and **end** are reserved words in POP2 and 'append' is the chosen name of the function. Then the function can be used and, as before,

append ("green", f) =>
**[red white blue green]

Notice the simplicity of this function definition, due to the ability to refer to a list as a whole, as compared with the similar operation written in Algol W.

Each element of the above lists is represented, as in Lisp, by a 'pair', i.e., two adjacent areas of store for the head of the element and for its tail (or, more precisely, for a pointer to the tail, which may be 'nil'). Although the contents and relationships of elements may change, the areas of store which hold their representations do not, and POP2 refers to these as *static lists*. By contrast, a *dynamic list* is one whose elements can be generated by an unambiguous rule or function and, therefore, need not all be stored explicitly. For instance, if n has the initial value -1, the positive integers can be represented by the function

function next; n+1 —> n; n **end**;

POP2 then provides a built-in function 'fntolist' which converts this rule into a dynamic list if and when required, after which the standard list operations are applicable. For example,

fntolist(next) —> x
hd(x) =>
** 1
hd(tl(x)) =>
** 2

A valuable application of a dynamic list in an interactive language occurs when a set of items is received from an input device and can be formed into a dynamic list to serve directly as the argument of a function.

A 'pair', used to represent an element of a static list, is a special case of a *record*. The definition of a record class, made by using the standard function 'recordfns', is similar in principle to a corresponding declaration in Algol W but includes only the name of the class and a list of integers; because no data types are assigned, the latter gives the number of bits required to store each component of the record (with zero representing one machine word). For example, the class 'student' with components name (one word), course code (two 6-bit characters) and mark (an integer less than 1000) may be defined as

recordfns ("student", [0,12,10])

The effect of this definition is to produce automatically a family of functions for handling the new class of records and place them on a system-maintained stack. This stack holds all values which result from expressions or functions until they are printed or assigned to a variable. The functions generated are, in order, a 'constructor' which creates an instance of the record class when given values of its component fields, the inverse 'destructor' which produces all the component fields given a record (but does not destroy the record), and a 'doublet' for each field to provide access to each (cf. the function 'hd' for a list-pair). (A doublet includes two functions, for read access and assign access respectively.)

In order to refer to the newly defined record class and invoke its associated functions, the user will assign these results of the function 'recordfns' to appropriate and previously declared variables (and thereby pop up the stack). For example:

recordfns ("student",[0,12,10]) $\rightarrow$ mark, $\rightarrow$ course, $\rightarrow$ name,
$\rightarrow$ splitst, $\rightarrow$ formst

Notice that the order of assignment is the reverse of the order of generation of the functions because of the mode of operation of a stack. Subsequently, some typical operations would be

formst("james","C2", 341) $\rightarrow$ stl;
mark(stl) + 59 $\rightarrow$ mark(stl);
if course (stl) = "C2" then total + 1 $\rightarrow$ total;

The records of this class are not linked, but linked structures can be created since any item of a record can refer to a list and each member of a list can be a record.

The method of creating new record classes shows that a function value can be assigned to a variable just as a numerical or structural value is assigned. Sometimes when a value is created or calculated, and therefore placed on the stack, it is not subsequently assigned to a variable — for example, because the result is to be printed but not stored. A nameless function for this purpose must be written as a 'lambda-expression' instead of a 'function definition' (which would cause the result to be assigned to a variable). For instance, a simple function which doubles a given integer is:

lambda i ; 2 * i end.

A lambda expression such as this may be necessary if a function is called, one of whose arguments must itself be a function. Suppose that a transformation f, whose exact form has not yet been stated, is to be applied to every element of a list p. A general function 'modify' can be defined as:

```
function modify p f; vars pl;
        p → pl;
  next: if not (null (pl)) then f(hd(pl)) —> hd(pl);
        tl(pl) —> pl;
        goto next    close
end;
```

Thereafter, given a list g of integers, every element can be doubled by the function call:

modify (g, lambda i ; 2* i end);

An array, like a list, can be represented explicitly or by a rule. An example of the latter method is the diagonal matrix represented by:

```
function diagonal i j;
        if i = j then 1 else 0 close
end;
```

Alternatively, an explicit representation is created by the standard function 'newarray' which takes two arguments: a list of bounds (alternatively lower and upper for each of n dimensions), and a function taking n arguments which initializes the values stored in the array. The latter function brings another opportunity for the use of a lambda-expression: as an illustration, the transpose of a given matrix a which has p rows and q colums is the matrix b created by:

newarray([% 1 q 1 p%] , lambda i j; a(j,i)end) —> b

(where decorated brackets must be used for the list of bounds, since q and p are expressions to be evaluated).

Array elements are referred to with subscripts in a perfectly standard way, as shown by a(j,i) in the creation of b, and all array operations can take place irrespective of whether the operands are represented explicitly or by rule. The net effect is that storage space for an array can, in the latter cases, be drastically reduced as compared with traditional representations, and that an array in POP2 can be regarded as a function rather than a data structure. This recalls the mathematical interpretation of an array as an operator.

POP2 contains a number of other features which are beyond the scope of a short survey, but the syntax of the language can, if necessary, be extended by the user in two ways. Firstly new syntax words can be defined as macros. The macro name is declared, followed by a list of statements which are thereafter incorporated in the program text at compile time wherever the macro is invoked. Only syntax words can be introduced in this way, as a macro in POP2 may not have any formal parameters. A second mode of extension allows new operators to be defined and given a suitable precedence level. For example, an inequality operator '/=' with precedence 7 (the range is from 1 to 9, with 1 the highest precedence) is declared and defined as follows:

> **vars operation** 7 /=;
> **lambda** x y ; **if** x = y **then** false **else** true **end** $->$ **nonop** /=;

where the reserved word 'nonop' acts like QUOTE in Lisp in preventing any attempt to evaluate the operator as it is being defined; at this point the operator is, in effect, an identifier to which a value is being assigned.

Simula
POP2 is an interactive language, but interaction of a different kind arises in simulation problems where a number of processes must cooperate or compete. A programming language for such problems must provide the means of describing the component processes, creating instances of each process which can coexist, and scheduling their execution in any chosen order. Once such facilities exist, the modular structure of the language tends to encourage the construction of a wide variety of application packages of which simulation is merely one.

Simula, which has evolved in this way, is a language which retains most of the syntax of Algol 60 but also includes an extended and generalized form of the record classes contained in Algol W and Pascal. The extended concept is known as a **class**, of which an **object** is a specific instance which is accessed by a **reference** variable. The crucial generalization is that a class may possess not only data attributes (a structure) but also operations to which it is relevant. For example, a class of 'complex number' has the attributes of coordinates, modulus, and amplitude, but it also has the operative attribute of conjugacy; a class of 'person' may include the attributes of name, age, sex, address and also the operation 'marry' (to form an **object** of a further class 'family') and the operation 'birthyear' (to calculate year of birth, knowing age and current calendar year). For example,

> **class** person (name, age, sex);
> **text** name; **integer** age; **boolean** sex;
> **begin boolean** adult;
>   **ref** (family) **procedure** marry . . .
>   **integer procedure** birthyear . . .
>   **if** age $>=$ 18 **then** adult := **true else** false;
> **end**;

Notice, from the use of 'adult' in the last line, that the value of an attribute can be initialized within the body of a class declaration. An object of any class is created by the syntax word **new**, and attributes of the object are referred to by concatenation. For example,

p1 := **new** person ("jones",20, T);
y := p1. birthyear (thisyear);

A class can possess attributes which are themselves classes, for example,
class family;
begin class father; . . .
    class mother; . . .
    class child; . . .

        . . .
end;

so that, if smith := **new** (family), it is possible to refer to the compound entity

smith.father

All attributes of the 'family' class can be incorporated as a package in a user program (concerned, say, with social statistics) merely by writing the class name as a prefix to the program block.

Equally, a class of objects can be defined in a nested manner, as, for instance,

class quadrilateral . . .

followed by the 'prefix class'

quadrilateral **class** parallelogram . . .

and

parallelogram **class** rectangle . . .

An object of one of these classes will then possess all attributes of its own class and its encompassing prefix class. Notice that, whereas a subset of a set implies a restriction of the membership, a subclass has a richer, more extensive range of attributes than its prefix class.

When an object of a class is generated by **new**, execution of the class body begins, with the necessary structures created and operations carried out. However, its execution can be suspended if the class body includes the procedure 'detach', an important feature which allows one activity to be 'frozen' (and resumed later) while another takes its place. As a result, a number of objects (of the same or different classes) can exist simultaneously and be executed in quasi-parallel mode as required for simulation problems. Other necessary attributes such as the maintenance of queues and sequencing of processes are defined in a prefix class 'simulation' which is available as a system package.

The degree to which a user can schedule the order of execution of a program is a distinctive contribution of Simula, and the class concept neatly combines the definition of a data structure with the description of operations on it. By use of prefix classes, a number of levels of programming can be created, where a user can deploy his specialist knowledge and skill with the aid of packages developed at the more detailed levels. It is this modularity in both definition and execution which gives Simula its value for application-package programming.

Algol 68

In one sense Algol 68 shares with PL/1 the objective of providing a universal programming tool, whatever the nature of the application, but this aim is approached in a very different way by providing a 'kit' consisting of a relatively small number of parts from which tools of almost infinite variety can be constructed, whereas PL/1 offers a very large but inextensible set of ready made tools. In other words, the design of Algol 68 aims to use a relatively small number of concepts for the description of data and operations, which can then be combined and interrelated with as few restrictions as possible. This principle, which can also be seen in Pascal, is known as 'orthogonal design'. Not only is such a language 'tidier' but it is easier for a user to understand and appreciate its principles and to exploit them to the full.

All the data types of Algol 68 have occurred in one or more other languages — numeric, character, and reference variables, strings, dynamic arrays, record structures, etc — but the concepts are unified and restrictions removed. When the type of an item of data cannot be confined to one possibility, the uncertainty is accepted, but its range must be defined by declaring a union of types: for example,

> **union** info (char, int, bool)

An important factor in achieving flexibility and clarity without confusion is the strict use of terminology on which the language is based. Indeed, just as Algol 60 was notable as much for its use of Backus—Naur form to express syntax concisely as for the power of the language itself, so one of the major contributions of Algol 68 may be the attention it gives to the nature and role of the objects being manipulated by a computer program.

A clear distinction is made between the *name* or *identifier* of an object, the *location* in which that object is represented, and the *value* of the object. For example, the integer declaration

> int i

although accepted as a shorthand, is not strictly accurate. It reserves a location for an object whose value (currently undefined) is of type or 'mode' integer, but the identifier i will be used to access and refer to this object, and hence is not itself an integer but a reference to an integer. A more accurate declaration of the

148

mode of i is therefore

ref int i

The object whose mode *is* 'integer' is the location to which i refers, which raises the question of how space is allocated in Algol 68. Two methods are used: a static allocation from a stack which gives variables a scope corresponding to the block structure of the program, as in Algol 60 and Algol W, and a dynamic allocation as in Algol W and Pascal from a system-maintained source of free space known as the **heap**, for structures such as records whose size cannot be determined at compile time. The space generator for the former case is the word **loc**, followed by the mode of the object for which space is required; in the case above this is

loc int

A strict declaration can now be completed by identifying the reference to a location and the location which has been allocated, obtaining

ref int i = **loc int**

Notice that this is an assertion of equality, not an assignment.

This declaration has been described in detail to introduce some terminology of Algol 68 (**mode, ref, heap**, etc) and also because it is important to be aware of the true nature of the actions involved if the language is to be used effectively. The concept of a location which can be accessed by a pointer is vital for dynamic structures, and Algol 68 is merely making this concept generally applicable so that, as promised, objects of any mode can be treated in a uniform manner.

Wherever possible, shorthand notations (such as the declaration **int** i) are accepted and automatically 'extended'. However, it is not always possible to omit the word **ref**: the format of an element of a simple list can be described by the mode declaration

mode simlist = **struct** (**char** datum, **ref simlist** link);

whereas

mode noton = **struct** (**char** datum, **noton** cell);

is illegal, because the recursive form of definition would mean that the format could never be completed. (A particular implementation of Algol 68 may also place some restrictions on the symbols such as simlist which can be used for new modes.)

An element of mode **simlist** can be created by the declaration

simlist e;

in which case e is a local variable. More appropriately, since **simlist** is potentially a dynamic structure, e can be given global scope by calling the heap generator:

ref simlist e = heap simlist;

or, briefly,

heap simlist e;

As elements of **simlist** are generated, any one of them can be accessed by a pointer, p, declared as

ref simlist p;

so that a new element can be generated on the heap and assigned to p by the statement

p := heap simlist;

Notice that the mode of p itself is **ref ref simlist**, because it refers to a location whose contents are to be interpreted as a reference to an element of mode **simlist.** (An alternative form of the last statement is **heap simlist** e; p:= e;).

Space which has been claimed from the heap is automatically recovered by a garbage collector which, when necessary, traces all accessible structures and sweeps up any remaining areas to replenish the heap.

Space for an array of fixed dimensions, for example

[1:5, 3:6] **real** a;

is allocated from the stack, and it is possible to refer to the array as a whole, e.g., read (a), and to individual elements such as a[2,5], and also to any 'slice' of the array, e.g. the middle three elements of the last column of a are written

a[2:4,6].

A slice is regarded as an array in its own right, but is indexed from one for each dimension, so that

a[2:4,6] [3]   is the element   a[4,6].

Alternatively, if b is a one-dimensional array having three elements, it may be more convenient to assign the slice as a whole to b:

b := a[2:4,6] ;

The elements of an array can be of any type, provided they are all the same, except another array. This means that a two-dimensional array, for example, must be declared as one unit (like a, above) and not as a row of columns or column of rows. However it is perfectly possible to set up a row (or column) of references, and the references can point to arrays. Suppose that a1, ... a4 are four two-dimensional arrays and that d is a one-dimensional array with four elements. The structure of Fig. 7.9 can be represented in which, in the strict terminology of Algol 68, the elements of d are of mode 'reference to real array

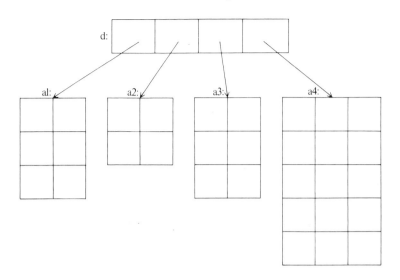

Fig. 7.9

of two dimensions' and hence the declaration of d is

[1:4] **ref** [,] **real** d;

This permits access to the subordinate arrays in two steps, whereas one step would have sufficed if the elements of d could themselves have been arrays. Notice that the subordinate arrays can be of different sizes provided they are all two-dimensional and real.

An array declared as

[m:n **flex**] **real** x;

is said to have a 'flexible upper bound', although it is initially indexed from m to n (where these are two integer variables whose values are known). In particular,

[1:0 **flex**] **char** s;

is a flexible vector which is initially empty, but which can be used for storing a string of characters of any length; the upper bound is adjusted as and when necessary: for example,

s :=   "a string of length 21";

makes the upper bound 21. A shorter declaration of s is

string s;

which is expanded automatically to the previous form.

It is obviously necessary to generate space for flexible arrays from the heap. But notice that if two strings, s1, s2, are concatenated to form a new single string,

>   s := s1 + s2;

then the spaces occupied by s1 and s2 cannot be collected as garbage, so long as s1 and s2 still refer to these areas. This can make string operations extravagant in store demands, unless obsolete strings are replaced by a null string, for example,

>   s1 := "␣";

Another facet of the consistent and uniform design of Algol 68 is that a variable (i.e., a reference to a location) is an object that can be produced by a function, just as any other object of a program can be produced. A simple example is the conditional clause

>   if b then x else y

where b is of mode boolean. If x and y have mode 'reference to real' then the result of the clause will also have this mode and hence a real value can be assigned to it:

>   if b then x else y := 0.1;

Conversely, a function is regarded by Algol 68 as just another value which can be assigned to a suitable variable (cf. functions in Lisp and POP2). If a binary tree has been defined as the mode

>   **mode bintree** = **struct** (**ref bintree** llink, **char** datum, **ref bintree** rlink);

then two procedures can be declared which yield the string of characters obtained by traversing a given binary tree T in preorder and symmetric order respectively:

>   **proc** preorder = (**bintree** T) string: . . .;
>   **proc** symorder = (**bintree** T) string: . . .;

If also the variable p is declared as

>   **ref proc (bintree) string** p;

then p can receive either the value 'preorder' or 'symorder' as required and subsequently be used to deliver the appropriate traversal, for example,

>   print (p(T)).

Similarly, a procedure can generate a value which is itself a procedure. A simple example is

>   **proc** trigfn = (**int** n) **proc** (**real**) **real**:
>   **begin case** n **in** sin, cos, tan **end**;

in which n is the formal parameter of the procedure 'trigfn', and the result of calling trigfn is another procedure which has a real parameter and produces a real result. The call

    x := trigfn(n)(theta)

stores in x the appropriate trigonometrical function of theta according to the selected value of n, for instance, cos (theta) if n = 2.

    An operator is another way of 'getting something done' which may be more convenient than the use of a procedure. In Algol 68 additional operators can be defined for variables of standard or user-defined modes, and priorities can be assigned. An operator declaration closely resembles a procedure declaration; for instance, the operator '+' can be defined as follows for the standard modes **string** and **compl** (i.e., complex, with fields 're' and 'im').

    op + = (**string** a, b) **string**:
            begin int m = **upb** a,   n = **upb** b;
                [1:m + n] **char** c;
                c[1:m] : = a;
                c[m + 1:m + n] : = b;
                c

        end;

    op + = (**compl** a, b) **compl**:
            ((**re of** a + **re of** b), (**im of** a + **im of** b));

and the priority of '+' is declared as

    priority + = 6;

Once declared in this way, a new operator can be used just like any standard operator. Note, however, that the operand modes must usually conform strictly to their specification in the declaration, as the routine to be associated with an operator often depends on its operands, as occurs for '+'. All monadic operators are given the top priority level, 10, but dyadic operators can have a priority anywhere in the range 1 to 9.

    There is no doubt that the very flexibility of Algol 68 requires a clarity of thought and agility of mind which can be unfamiliar to those accustomed to less strict languages, but it is an interesting fact that students without experience of other languages find Algol 68 straightforward in expression and not difficult to learn. Because of its ability to express very general forms of structures and of operation, it has already proved its value in systems programming, and it seems certain that its concepts, at least, will significantly influence the next few years of software development.

Bliss

System software translates instructions written in a machine-independent code into a form applicable to a particular system of hardware, but, by contrast, the translation process itself has rarely been expressed in a machine-independent manner. Bliss, though based on the features of the PDP10 computer, is designed primarily to encourage an independent description, and gain for systems programmers the advantages of ease of expression, amendment, and transferability which high-level languages have long provided for the general user.

A major problem to be faced is that many system programs are, by their nature, in continual demand, whereas any user's program is merely one amongst many. The efficiency of system software is therefore of the utmost importance, and this in turn implies not only 'tight' coding but also the ability to exploit all the hardware features of a particular configuration. Hardware influences data representation in the manner in which space is allocated — how many bits for a character, how many fields in a computer word, total capacity of store — and also in the most suitable methods of access to a structure: for instance, the availability of fast indexing registers or the existence of bit operations for flag indicators.

A central feature of Bliss is that the declaration of a structure includes not only its name and access parameters, but also a specification of the access formula to be used; for example, an array structure, with 8 rows and 10 columns, stored by rows, is declared as

structure array $[i,j] = (.array + 10* i + j)$;

where '.array' gives the location of the first element of the array area and both indices run from zero upwards. By this means the mode of access to a structure is separated from the description of operations to be carried out on its elements, so that either can be modified without affecting the other. If it should prove more convenient to index both dimensions of the array structure from one upwards, and to store the elements by columns, the structure declaration is rewritten as

structure array $[i,j] = (.array + (i-1) + 8(j-1))$;

A structure declaration defines an access formula, but an area or 'segment' of space is reserved by an 'allocation' declaration: for example,

local x[80] ,y[80] ;

This space is not tied to a particular type of data, but can have an access algorithm imposed on it by a 'map' declaration: for example,

map array x:y;

and x and y will now be interpreted as representing structures of type 'array'. A typical operation on the structures is the assignment statement

x[.a,.b] ← y [.a,.b] ;

and the form of this instruction is quite unaffected by the choice of structure declaration.

Space for all data in Bliss is allocated in 'segments' which are one or more machine words in length; a consecutive set of bits within a segment is a 'field', which may be named by a pointer. The language contains no data types, and all data are treated as patterns of bits, though a structure may be defined by the user. The scope of an identifier may be declared as local or global, and it is possible to allocate space in registers by a declaration of the form

register r1, r2;

Like Algol 68, Bliss makes a careful distinction between a value, the location in which that value is held, and the identifier of the location. It is the last of these which is defined by an allocation declaration such as

local x[80];

or

global n;

so that n is interpreted as a pointer to its allocated segment and x as a pointer to the first word of its segment area. The notation for 'the contents of' an identifier such as n, i.e. the address to which n refers, is '.n'. Similarly '. . n' means 'the contents of the location .n', i.e. the current value of n, and '. . x' means the value contained in the first word of x. The contents of the second word of x can be obtained by

. . t   where   t ← .x+1

or, more briefly, by

.(.x+1)

since the result of any expression is treated as a pointer value if the dot operator is applied to it.

Again like Algol 68, every expression in Bliss computes a value, so that there are no statements in the sense of Algol or Fortran. The language provides control expressions and simple expressions, where the latter include arithmetic, boolean, bit, shift, and field-access expressions. Since no data types are specified, the interpretation of any bit pattern is a function of the operator and not the operand — the opposite of most languages. Control expressions do not include a general 'goto' in order to clarify the structure and meaning of a program, but the conditional, case, loop, and function (call) expressions all take familiar forms. There is also a select expression:

select e **of nset** e_0 :f_0 ;e_1 :f_1 ;. . .e_n :f_n **tesn**

in which the second component f_i of a pair is executed for every pair whose first component e_i has the same value as e; this allows the investigation of all cases relevant to a condition — as required, for instance, in the analysis of syntax. Each of these control expressions influences an environment of one or more expressions, but a set of escape expressions (one for each type of environment) allows execution of the environment to be terminated prematurely if appropriate.

Bliss also provides simple macro facilities which enable a user to assign names to particular bit patterns and to compound expressions. Nested macro calls are allowed, though not recursive calls or nested definitions. By using macros, bit patterns can be classified and operations clarified, but there cannot be any automatic type checking as provided in languages such as Algol.

It will be clear that Bliss is a very much less ambitious language than the general-purpose languages described earlier in this chapter. This is not surprising, since it must take a much more detailed view of the execution process and could be regarded more as a high-level assembly language. (It does contain features, not described here, which are machine dependent.) The absence of data types again recalls assembly languages, but the powerful structure and map declarations which Bliss contains allow a user to interpret a storage area in any appropriate manner. More generally, programs written in a language such as Bliss in preference to assembly code have a more logical and coherent structure, which in turn makes them very much easier to document, to develop, and to communicate.

Problems

7.1 Show how a two-dimensional Fortran array can be used to represent the structure of a binary tree. Write down an algorithm in terms of this representation for traversing the binary tree in preorder.

(The algorithm need not be expressed formally as a Fortran program.)

7.2 Is there any equivalent in Cobol of a pointer or reference variable, and if so, what is it called? If there is no equivalent type, why is this?

7.3 What advantage can be gained by using STATIC storage allocation in a PL/1 program?

7.4 The following definitions are made in a Pascal program. Describe in words the structures w,x,y,z.

```
type person = record    name: array[1..12] of char;
                        refno: integer;
                        dept: (admin, finance, sales, despatch);
               end;
type w = array [1..20] of ↑person;
type x = file of person;
type y = file of x;
type z = array [1..4] of y;
```

7.5 What is the effect of the Lisp function EQUAL defined as follows:

```
(EQUAL, (LAMBDA, (X, Y),
                    (COND, ((ATOM,X),(EQ,X,Y)),
                           ((ATOM,Y),NIL),
                           ((EQUAL, (CAR,X),(CAR, Y)),
                               (EQUAL, (CDR,X), (CDR,Y))),
                           (T,NIL) )))
```

How does EQUAL differ from the elementary function EQ? Are there any circumstances in which it would be impossible to evaluate the function EQUAL?

7.6 Consider the Lisp function APPEND, defined below.

```
(LABEL,APPEND,(LAMBDA,(X,Y),
                (COND,((NULL,X),Y),
                      (T,(CONS,(CAR,X),(APPEND,(CDR,X),Y))) )))
```

Given that the initial arguments are the lists (P,Q,R) and (S,T,U) respectively, write down each stage in the recursive evaluation of the function, showing the current state of the 'association list' (i.e., the stack associating values of formal parameters and actual parameters). Verify that the result is the list (P,Q,R,S,T,U).

There is a logical weakness in the definition of APPEND as given. What is it, and how could it be removed?

7.7 Given that the function APPEND is available as a system function in Lisp, show how it can be used to define a recursive function INVERSE which will reverse the order of the elements of a list, including any sublists: for example,

(INVERSE,(QUOTE,(A,(B,C),D,E))) → (E,D,(C,B),A)

7.8 In what ways will the absence of data types in POP2 affect a user of the language? What is the relationship in POP2 between functions and data?

7.9 What are the 'attributes' of a class in a Simula program?
     Distinguish between the following Simula structures:

```
(a)   class A (param1);        (b)   class C (param3);
         begin                          begin class D(param4);
            .                                  begin
            .                                     .
            .                                     .
         end;                                     .
      A class B (param2)                       end;
         begin                          end;
            .
            .
         end;
```

7.10 Suppose we wish to define a class of REAL objects and a class of COMPLEX objects in a Simula program. Which class should be the prefix class? Give examples of attributes which each class might possess.

7.11 Suppose that the 'sum' of two binary trees A and B is defined as the binary tree T which has A as its left subtree and B as its right subtree. Write down in Algol 68 a definition of the operator '+' so that its use can be extended in this way to apply to the mode **bintree** as defined in this chapter.

7.12 Define in Algol 68 a mode **table** such that each entry in the table consists of two **string** fields called 'key' and 'content', and the size of an instance of this mode can be determined at runtime.

How would you amend your definition if the 'content' field may be either a string value or a reference to a table of overflow entries?

When a variable T of mode **table** is declared, would it be more appropriate to write

      table T   or   **heap table** T ?

How should space be allocated for overflow entries?

7.13 Compare the data types available in Algol W with those available in Algol 68; use the notation of Algol 68 to describe the data types of Algol W.

(Cambridge, 1974)

8. The interaction of data attributes and structure

The description of 'a set of information' is necessarily based on names or values assigned to certain subsets or attributes of the set, and these names not only convey facts about their own attributes but also act as points of reference for the description of relationships which, as shown in chapter 1, are an integral part of 'information'. Subsequent chapters, in considering the representation of information, have emphasized this structural aspect. But stored information is of value only if it can be retrieved and used; from this point of view, its structure is merely a tool which enables the required aspects of the information content to be reached and retrieved. For instance, 'find all the descendants of Queen Victoria', or 'list all towns in Great Britain whose population exceeds 500 000', or 'what are the associated companies of XYZ Ltd?'.

Structure can therefore be regarded in two ways: as a property of data, and as a means of access to data. This is rather similar to the dual view of the triangle in Fig. 8.1, which can be described as a set of three points X,Y,Z which possess (are joined by) three lines, or as a set of three lines, a,b,c, which lead to (intersect at) three points.

Descriptions of data

Traditionally, computer languages have provided the *means* for linking related items within a set of information, but have placed on the user the responsibility for specifying what relationships actually exist. This approach encourages a structural view of information as a hierarchy (when Cobol-like languages are

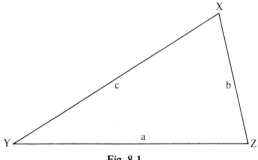

Fig. 8.1

	Name	Company ref. no.	Branch
$R_1 \equiv$ employee			

	Item	Quantity	Unit price	Branch
$R_2 \equiv$ stock				

Fig. 8.2

used) or as a network (using linked records). Just as the user specifies the structural relationships of the data, so an access path must be stated whenever a reference is made to any item within the data; this may involve a subscripted element in an array, or a qualified reference in a Cobol or PL/1 structure, or an algorithm for a dynamic chain in a record structure. In other words, the description of operations on a set of information requires awareness of the storage representation of that structure.

This is rather like saying that the use of real (i.e., non-integer) arithmetic requires knowledge of the details of floating-point representation. Knowledge of the storage structure does, of course, provide additional information such as numerical accuracy or speed of access, but the description of operations on data is more logically based on its natural structure alone. This is the basis of the 'relational' model of data (see Childs (1968) and Codd (1970)): given information which consists of sets of data $S_1, S_2, \ldots, S_n$, a relation on these sets, $R(S_1, S_2, \ldots, S_n)$, is a set of 'n-tuples' $(s_1, s_2, \ldots, s_n)$ such that $s_i \in S_i$. For example, the relations 'employee' and 'stock' could be represented by the tables in Fig. 8.2. Operations on the data are set operations which produce new relations; for example, union, intersection, difference, join (which amalgamates two relations which have a common 'domain' or attribute), and projection (in which some attributes are ignored and any duplicate members which then appear are removed from the set). Furthermore, a relation is an unordered set (the form of its storage structure is irrelevant) so that a new member may be added at any time or an obselete member deleted. A relational model of data enables questions to be posed in a natural way and readily transformed into set operations without the need for the user to know how the sets themselves have been represented (although a storage allocation system must, of course, exist).

More generally, the representation of any set of information can be considered in the manner of Fig. 8.3. There is good reason to separate the description of data from the definition of algorithms which access the elements concerned, just as the latter can be separated from the details of store allocation. In this way, levels of programming can develop, each of which is to a large extent independent of

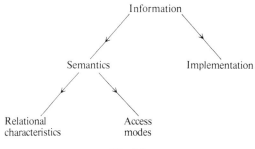

Fig. 8.3

changes in the others. But although a number of high-level languages provide facilities for the description of access algorithms, there has been little progress as yet towards implementing relational descriptions of data. Some indication of the problems involved can be gained from the difficulty of accessing an inverted file, which can be regarded as one relation; most relational models involve not one but a number of such relations.

Despite the difficulties, there is little doubt that the emphasis on data description will grow as a result of the increasing size and complexity of the information being stored — the database concept. A typical picture of the flow of information which faces a systems analyst is shown in Fig. 8.4, and it is essential that the method adopted to represent the information should be sufficiently flexible to accommodate the inevitable changes that will occur in response to trading conditions, staff turnover, government regulations, etc., without the need for major reassessment of the underlying implementation.

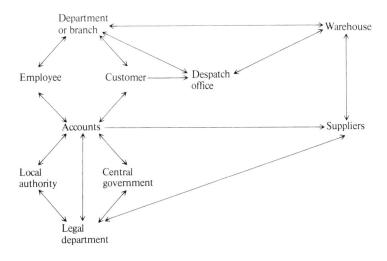

Fig. 8.4   Typical information flow

The CODASYL proposals (1971), suggest the use of two types of languages: a data-definition language (DDL), which describes the overall logic of a database, and if necessary renames the subset of features which are of interest to specific users; and a data-manipulation language (DML) containing commands which are added to a host language (Cobol, Fortran, Algol, etc.) to enable the database to be accessed and modified. The objective is to have a common DDL which can be interpreted by a number of DML's, each of which extends an existing high-level language. The DDL describes the database as it is, and does not include any means of specifying set operations by which the database can be reconfigured; all operations, whether for access or amendment, must be specified at the more detailed and storage-dependent level of the DML. By comparison with the relational view of data, the DDL demands a more specific description of the natural structure of the information, and it is written in a form reminiscent of the data division of a Cobol program. The database is therefore seen as a network (not necessarily as a hierarchy) with the emphasis on its structure rather than its attributes. Yet, however important structure may be – and this book has been largely concerned with its representation – it is usually inherent in information rather than explicitly stated; therefore the attributes of data form the more natural base for its description. The cost to be paid is the difficulty of subsequent implementation.

Management of large data sets
An important factor in the use of a large database is that it will be interrogated by a number of users and their optimum methods of access may well conflict. The system must therefore have a supervisor or administrator whose responsibility is to accept amendments, authorize deletions, and monitor the modes of use of the data, so that it can be organized to provide the greatest overall benefit. The task is analogous to the operating system in a multi-access programming environment, but the time scale of operation is very much longer. The administrator is an individual, not a programming system, who decides on the interconnections which are to be represented in the database, the location and method of storage of files, and sets up a static base accordingly. The individual user is at liberty to extract data from this base and set up his own structures which may grow dynamically, but the global structure is changed only by the conscious intervention of the administrator.

This view of data management once again emphasizes structure, and implies that the likely patterns of access to the data, and hence the links which should be incorporated, are well known. If this is not the case, many of the links will be provided on a speculative basis and are likely to prove either redundant or inadequate, but as programming effort is invested in the structure which has been chosen, modification of the structure becomes increasingly difficult.

A more flexible approach, suggested by Stocker and Dearnley (1973) is to allow the system itself to monitor patterns of access and create versions of a 'folio' or set of information whose structures are determined by use. The system is given the ability to create and access a number of standard file structures and to select the key on which a file should be ordered. One folio of data may lead to more than one file if the pattern of use makes duplication worthwhile. The 'cost' of any enquiry is measured by the number of disc accesses likely to be required, and it is a fundamental feature of the system that this cost estimate is given to a user before the answer to the enquiry is initiated. The estimate may be accepted or rejected; in the latter case it may be left pending and may be initiated later if a reorganization of the data reduces the cost of the enquiry. Reorganization can take place as a direct result of an accepted estimate, or because the system, in monitoring requests, detects that a new structure would be of value to a number of users.

This system is intended primarily for a database which is large but has relatively infrequent and unpredictable use; a longer response time is traded for a reduction in storage costs, obtained (even though duplication may exist) by minimizing the number of relationships which are represented. Rather like a relational model, the prime importance is placed on the attributes of data, and relationships are constructed only as they are required.

Associative storage

The machine-level equivalent of describing a set of information in terms of its entities rather than its structure is to access data by content of location instead of by reference to location (using 'reference' with a meaning similar to that of Algol 68). Suppose that the problem is to obtain all records containing a particular field value X: then, instead of following a previously created chain linking all such records, the relevant field of every record is matched against X and the record as a whole accepted if the match is successful.

In a content-addressed storage structure, pointers are in general unnecessary, since any required links will be established by the content of a record. For example, if a man has two sons, then a record representing the man contains their names but does not contain pointers to the two records representing the sons. If required, the latter records will be obtained by identifying the content of their 'name' fields. The only exception where pointers may occur is if a 'summary' of a record is maintained separately from the full record, the summary containing a pointer to the full record together with those fields which may be used as access keys. In this case the summary would be accessed associatively, but the full record would then be retrieved by the reference pointer. The selection of certain keys for the summary does, of course, restrict the interconnections of the structure to these fields, but within this limitation any associations can be made and the summary records can be held on a significantly smaller device than the full database — a possible factor of ten has been suggested.

A scheme on these lines, for a database of order 100 megabytes, has been proposed by Colouris et al. (1972), though there is as yet no generally available hardware for the associative access device. The scheme suggested would use two rotating stores, one for the full database, conventionally accessed, and one for the associatively addressed summary store. The latter would be continuously scanned by arranging for its data to stream past a bank of 'comparator' units, each of which can hold a key-field value. The output from each unit is a pattern of one or more bits, indicating the result of the associative comparison, and for each record these patterns can be combined by boolean operators in an 'evaluation unit' according to the access criteria, e.g., 'a student who is male, over 21, and studying geography'. If the criteria are satisfied, the pointer in the summary is used to retrieve the full record in a standard manner. It is suggested that the whole of the summary store should be tested against a minimum of twenty keys in one second, which implies a data rate of approximately 10^9 bits/second for a single stream of data or correspondingly less if parallel servicing is possible; this is comparable to the performance of existing direct-access devices. Amendments to the database can be made without difficulty by accessing the record and its summary in the same manner as before and then carrying out a write operation for each (for this purpose only the locations in the summary store must be numbered). Since no structural pointers exist, these operations cannot vitiate any information held in other areas of the database, and similarly the store allocation can also be rearranged at will if this is necessary to avoid overwriting existing data.

When data are accessed associatively, the problem is to 'spot' a matching field wherever it occurs in the set of records. In theory these tests can and should be made simultaneously for every record in the set, since there is no reason for the records to be ordered in any way, as would be necessary for structurally accessed data.

An associatively addressed record consists of field symbols or names (normally but not exclusively alphanumeric), field delimiters, and record delimiters, in the form

$$(f_1, f_2, \ldots, f_n)$$

If both fields and records can be of variable length, the steps necessary to access all instances of a particular field value, say F_i, are

1 find and mark all opening record delimiters, '(';
2 find and mark the $(i-1)$th field delimiter following each of (1);
3 find and mark all fields immediately following (2) and such that $f_i = F_i$.

Unfortunately, the conventional von Neumann computer design has no provision for parallel access to the store as a whole, and the variable-length associative characteristics of data structures have been almost entirely ignored in hardware developments.

The first step towards parallel execution, as suggested by Beaven and Lewin (1972), is a common instruction highway connected to every location in the store (where a 'location' must now be regarded as the area needed to store one symbol). In a conventional design, the contents of a location would be moved to a central unit for processing, but parallel processing in this manner would imply the need for a data highway as wide as the store. Instead, the processing can be 'brought to the store' if each location is a 'cell' which not only stores a symbol but also contains a basic processing capability. Since the associative access essentially involves only symbol comparisons, the logic needed in each cell is not too complex. The result of each associative test must also be recorded and this, too, can be most conveniently included as one or more bits within a cell. Beaven and Lewin call this the 'activity' of the cell. Besides being retained as an attribute of the cell, this result can also be placed on a common output highway where the logical sum of the signals is formed. Notice that the activity or inactivity of individual cells partitions the store (as required by steps (a) and (b) above) for succeeding instructions.

This type of design has good potential for processing information of the database type in a more natural and efficient way, but it is not of universal value; the traditional von Neumann model remains excellent for fast numerical calculations and 'pipeline' models which combine conventional store access with a capability for parallel processing can handle array operations very efficiently.

Software developments
Whatever the architecture of a computer system, it has become accepted that it can be used effectively (bearing in mind the cost of both the system and human resources) only through the intervention of a programming language, usually at a 'high level'. However, it is an unresolved problem whether such languages should also vary with the nature of the application or whether a true general-purpose design can be found.

List- and string-processing facilities, at one time restricted to specialized languages such as Lisp, have now been incorporated in more convenient forms in other languages like Algol W and PL/1, so that changes in the structure of data can be represented almost as readily as changes in its content. However, from the structural point of view, these are 'low-level' languages, for the user must always be aware of the state of the structure in order to describe operations on it. Nor is it possible, when using these languages, to regard a variable structure as a single entity or data type, with operators which act on it as a unit to produce results which may themselves be structured entities.

By contrast, in Algol 68, and to a more limited extent in PL/1, the definitions of the standard arithmetic operators can be extended to arrays, so that operations such as their sum or product can be described as concisely as for scalars. The extended definitions must, of course, include a check on the compatibility of the array operands for the operation stated. Similarly new unary operators can be defined for arrays, such as transpose and inverse. These new definitions not only extend the scope of the language as a whole, but they also merge naturally with the basic syntax when this is appropriate: if a is a scalar, and x and y are row and column vectors respectively (of the same length), then the expression

x*y*a

has a quite meaningful scalar result.

There is no reason, in principle, why a language should not be extended in a similar way to express set operations (as distinct from element operations) on a database having the form of a digraph or network, but the problems are greater because the rules of compatibility are less rigid and the potential relationships more complex. Indeed, the dynamic nature of the structure may demand that new modes may be created dynamically by the execution of a mode-valued routine, so that the *type* of a structure (not merely its elements or links) can vary – e.g., a linear list, a circular list, or a two-way list. This is a feature beyond the scope of Algol 68, in which a procedure may produce a procedural value (a dynamically defined operation) but modes can only be defined statically. The definition of new modes must be accompanied by the definition of operators to act on them. Some of these are entirely unrelated to existing syntax – for example, the array operator 'transpose' has no scalar equivalent – but when corresponding semantics can occur (for instance, assignment) it is very desirable that the same symbol be used so that the language is extended in a natural way and diagnostic information is more easily produced. As already stated, this implies that an operator may be associated with a number of routines each corresponding to particular combinations of operands, the appropriate routine being selected, in general, at compile time. If dynamic modes can occur, then either selection must be delayed until run time or, more effectively, routines may be associated with a union of the possible modes.

The ability to define new modes and operators is a significant advance, making it possible to create programming units which are appropriate to specific applications and hence to describe algorithms in a more logical and problem-oriented manner. The user need not be aware of the precise representation of the data structure at every stage of execution, as he must when only basic structural operations are available. Nevertheless, the user must be sufficiently familiar with the ways in which aggregate operations can be based on the 'primitive' types and operations of the basic language to be able to make the new definitions he requires.

The question is whether even this degree of programming knowledge should be expected of the general user who, though he may be an expert accountant, draughtsman, mathematician, or musician, is not a software expert. Instead, should there be a series of languages, each tailored to their individual problems and knowledge? The difficulty then is that those working in an interdisciplinary field can find no language which contains all the facilities they need. Back to the general-purpose goal once more! A possible answer is some form of 'very-high-level' language in which both the database and operations on it can be expressed on a set-theoretic basis, and heuristic methods are used in developing storage representations which can respond dynamically to a wide and unpredictable variety of objectives. In other words, a language in which all the emphasis is placed on what is to be done rather than on how it is to be carried out. It is a challenging problem, but if it can be solved efficiently, the resulting simplification of structural programming problems will be similar to the simplification achieved for arithmetic problems by the advent of the first high-level algorithmic languages. And, in sheltering computer users from details of hardware operation, it will continue an emancipation which began with the use of symbolic addresses in assembly languages.

Problems

8.1 Reconsider the data of Problem 1.13 and set up a suitable relational model. Express the typical problems posed in the question as set operations on the relations you have chosen.

8.2 Describe an instruction set which would be appropriate for a computer which uses an associatively addressed storage system. State clearly the assumptions you make about the processing ability, if any, of the individual cells (which hold one character each) and the output channels available.

8.3 Which of the following has the highest priority and which the lowest?

'High-level languages should be designed to suit the user.'
'High-level languages should be designed to suit the hardware.'
'Hardware should be designed to suit the needs of high-level languages.'

(St Andrews, 1972)

8.4 What features and operations would you expect in a high-level structural programming language (i.e., a language related to structural algorithms as Algol is related to numerical algorithms).

8.5 You are engaged in the teaching of data structures, and you want to design an interactive software package which would allow students to test and run their algorithms for manipulating certain list structures. The package should be able to handle linear lists, circular lists, and doubly linked lists; it would run interpretively.

Describe in an essay form, with suitable diagrams wherever necessary, the design details of such a package. You should consider the following points:

(a) the type of statements you would allow your students to use in their algorithms;
(b) the method of storage for the programs the students type in;
(c) the organization of core in your package;

(d)   the interrogation facilities you would allow the students to have for the investigation of the workings of their algorithms;

(e)   the editing facilities you would allow the package to have.

(You are not expected to be concerned with the details of the interpreter itself, which you may consider as a black box.)

(Brighton Polytechnic, 1974)

Appendix

Notes on Algol W

The following notes refer to points at which Algol W differs slightly from the corresponding features of Algol 60. A description of Algol 60 can be found in Shepherd (1972), and readers interested in the formal definition of the two languages can consult Eve (1972) and the *Revised Algol Report* (Bauer, 1963).

1. Program structure

1.1 The outermost block of an Algol W program must be terminated by a full stop after END.

1.2 A block may or may not include declarations, i.e. a 'compound statement' is regarded as a block. This does not affect the scope of an identifier. Thus Fig. 3.2 contains three blocks, with declarations made in two of them.

1.3 The controlled variable of a 'for' statement need not be declared; it is 'defined' by its position immediately following the basic symbol FOR, but its scope is restricted to the statement following DO.

1.4 A label need not be declared; it is 'defined' by its position preceding a colon symbol, and its scope is the block in which its definition occurs.

1.5 Logical variables are declared as type LOGICAL (not Boolean).

2. Input/output

The assumed media are punched-card input and lineprinter output, and standard procedures are provided by the system for this purpose.

2.1 READ/WRITE inputs/outputs a set of values, beginning the set on a new card or new output line.

2.2 READON/WRITEON are similar, but continue from the position reached on a card or line at the end of a previous operation.

2.3 READCARD transmits 80 characters from a card without analysing them, and assigns them to a STRING variable of length 80.

2.4 These five procedures may be given any number of parameters.

2.5 For output, INTEGER and REAL numbers are right justified in a field of 14 characters and followed by two spaces; strings are printed in a field of exactly the string length.

(A string constant is indicated in an output statement by enclosing it in double quotes, as shown in the examples.)

3. Operators

The complete table of precedence beginning with the highest priority is:

LONG	SHORT	ABS				
**	SHL	SHR				
* /	DIV	REM				
+ −						
<	< =	>	> =	=	¬=	IS
¬						
AND						
OR						

ABS is the modulus operator.

LONG, SHORT convert floating point numbers between double precision and the standard single precision.

SHL, SHR operate on bit strings (Shift Left/Right).

DIV gives the quotient of integer division and REM gives the remainder
    e.g. 11 DIV 3 = 3   ;   11 REM 3 = 2.

IS is defined in chapter 3.

4. Iteration statements

These statements may use either the symbol WHILE or the symbol FOR. Note in the latter case that the control identifier must have an INTEGER value.

4.1   A WHILE statement has the form

WHILE ⟨logical expression⟩ DO ⟨statement⟩

4.2   A FOR statement has the form

FOR ⟨control identifier⟩ := ⟨list of integer expressions⟩
                                                         DO ⟨statement⟩

or

FOR ⟨control identifier⟩ := ⟨integer expression⟩ STEP
                              ⟨increment⟩ UNTIL ⟨limit⟩ DO ⟨statement⟩

4.21   The value of the control identifier may not be changed by the statement which follows DO.

4.22   Increment and limit are integer expressions which are evaluated and stored before entry to the statement which follows DO. The increment may not have the value zero.

4.23   'STEP ⟨increment⟩' may be omitted when increment has the value 1.

5. Arrays

5.1   The type of all arrays must be specified (REAL is not a default option).

5.2   Round brackets (not square) are used in all references to arrays and their elements.

5.3   In an array declaration, lower and upper bounds are separated by a repeated colon.

5.4   In an array declaration, all arrays must have the same bounds; however more than one declaration can be made. For example,

    INTEGER ARRAY K(1 :: 8);
    REAL ARRAY L,M(1 :: 4, 1 :: 5);
    REAL ARRAY N(1 :: 4, 1 :: 7);

6. Conditional statements

The IF statement is similar to Algol 60, but the **switch** declaration of Algol 60 is replaced by the use of a CASE statement. This has the form

    CASE ⟨integer expression⟩ OF
        BEGIN S1; S2; . . . SK END;

If ⟨integer expression⟩ has the value i, control goes to statement Si; if i lies outside the range (1,K) a fatal error occurs.

7. Procedures

7.1   Formal parameters of a procedure are specified in a procedure heading by a formal parameter list which immediately follows the procedure identifier: for example, a procedure to interchange two values:

        PROCEDURE CHANGE (REAL X,Y);

7.2   When a formal parameter is an array, the bounds are not specified, but each dimension of the array is indicated by an asterisk: e.g., the heading of a procedure SUM which calculates the row sum vector V of an array A with M rows and N columns would be

        PROCEDURE SUM (INTEGER M,N;
                        REAL ARRAY V($*$); REAL ARRAY A($*$,$*$));

7.3   A formal parameter may be called 'by value' only if the parameter is a simple variable — in particular, an array parameter may not be called by value.
        Call by value is indicated by VALUE following the type specification: for example,

        PROCEDURE SUM (INTEGER VALUE M,N;
                        REAL ARRAY V($*$); REAL ARRAY A($*$,$*$)).

7.4   Simple parameters may also be called 'by result' or 'by value result': for example,

        INTEGER VALUE RESULT M,N;

The use of RESULT, like VALUE, introduces a variable local to the procedure when the procedure is invoked. When VALUE is used, the value of the corresponding actual parameter is assigned to the local variable on entry to the procedure; when RESULT is used, the value of the local variable is assigned to the corresponding actual parameter on exit from the procedure.

Bibliography

Books

Berztiss, A. T. (1975) *Data Structures – Theory and Practice*, 2nd Edn, Academic Press, London.

Burstall, R. M., Collins, J. S., and Popplestone, R. J. (eds.) (1972) *Programming in POP2*, Edinburgh U. P., Edinburgh.

Elson, M. (1973) *Concepts of Programming Languages*, Science Research Associates, London.

Foster, J. M. (1967) *List Processing*, Macdonald, London.

Harrison, M. C. (1972) *Data Structures and Programming*, Scott, Foresman, Glenview, Illinois.

Iliffe, J. K. (1972) *Basic Machine Principles*, 2nd edn, Macdonald, London.

Knuth, D. E. (1973) *The Art of Computer Programming*, Vol. 1, 2nd Edn, Addison-Wesley, London.

Lindsey, C. H., and van der Meulen, S. G. (1971) *Informal Introduction to Algol 68*, North Holland, Amsterdam.

Page, E. S. and Wilson, L. B. (1973) *Information Representation and Manipulation in a Computer*, Cambridge U.P., Cambridge.

Shepherd, R. F. (1972) *Algol 60 Programming*, McGraw-Hill, London.

Weissman, C. (1968) *Lisp 1.5 Primer*, Dickenson Publishing Inc., Encino, CA.

Papers and reports

Bauer, H., *et al.*, (1963) 'Revised report on the algorithmic language Algol 60', *Comm. A.C.M.* **6**, 1.

Beaven, P. A. and Lewin, D. W., (1972). 'An associative parallel processing system for non-numerical computation', *Comp. J.*, **15**, 343

Childs, D. L., (FJCC 1968) 'Description of a set-theoretic data structure', *AFIPS Conference Proc.*, **33** (1), 557.

Codasyl Committee (1971), Report of the Data Base Task Group, Assoc. Comp. Machinery.

Codd, E. F., (1970) 'A relational model of data for large shared data banks', *Comm. A.C.M.*, **13**, 377.

Colouris, G. F., Evans, J. M. and Mitchell, R. W., (1972) 'Towards content-addressing in data bases', *Comp.J.* **15**, 95.

Dearnley, P. A., (1974) 'A model of a self-organising data management system', *Comp.J.* **17**, 13.

D'Imperio, M. E., (1969) 'Data structures and their representation in storage', *Ann.Rev.Auto.Prog.* **5**, 1.

Earley, J. (1971) 'Towards an understanding of data structures', *Comm.A.C.M.* **14**, 617.

Eve, J. (1972) *Algol W programming manual*, University of Newcastle on Tyne.

Hansen, W. J. (1969) 'Compact list representation: definition, garbage collection, and system implementation', *Comm.A.C.M.* **12**, 499.

Ichbiah, J. D., and Morse, S. P. (1972) 'General concepts of the SIMULA 67 programming language', *Ann.Rev. Auto. Prog.* **7**, 65.

Inglis, J., (1974) 'Inverted indexes and multi-list structures', *Comp.J.* **17**, 59.

Lindsey, C. H., (1972) 'Algol 68 with fewer tears', *Comp.J.* **15**, 176.

McCarthy, J., (1960) 'Recursive functions of symbolic expressions and their computation by machine', *Comm. A.C.M.* **3**, 184.

Schorr, H. and Waite, W. M., (1967) 'An efficient machine-independent procedure for garbage collection', *Comm.A.C.M.* **10**, 501:

Stocker, P. M. and Dearnley, P. A., (1973) 'Self-organising data management systems', *Comp. J.,* **16**, 100.

Vose, M. R., and Richardson, J. S., (1972) 'An approach to inverted index maintenance', *Comp. Bulletin* **16**, 256.

Wegbreit, B., (1972) 'A generalised compactifying garbage collector', *Comp.J.* **15**, 204.

Wegbreit, B., (1974) 'The treatment of data types in EL1', *Comm.A.C.M.* **17**, 251.

Wirth, N., (November 1972) 'The programming language Pascal' (Revised report), *Eidgenössiche Technische Hochschule*, Zürich.

Wulf, W. A., *et al.*, (1970) 'Bliss reference manual', Dept. of Computer Science, Carnegie Mellon University.

Index